# Jo Seagar's New Zealand Country Cookbook

## DEDICATION

*Dedicated to my mother, Fay Wellwood, with fondest love*

First published in 1993 by
TANDEM PRESS
2 Rugby Road, Birkenhead, Auckland 10
New Zealand

Copyright © 1993 text Jo Seagar
Copyright © 1993 photographs Greg Webb

Reprinted in paperback 1995, 1998, 1999

ISBN 0 908884 56 7

Production and design by Suellen Allen
Typesetting by Typocrafters
Styling by Suellen Allen
Photography by Greg Webb
Printed in Hong Kong by Everbest Printing Co

# JO SEAGAR'S
# NEW ZEALAND
# COUNTRY
# COOKBOOK

TANDEM

# ACKNOWLEDGEMENTS

My sincere appreciation and thanks to my photographer Greg Webb. Special thanks also to Bob Ross, my publisher; Renée Lang for all her editorial help; Suellen Allen for her art direction and design of this book; Robyn Langwell, editor of *North And South* (who gave me my first break in food writing) and its art director Voyteck Grzymala for his friendship and assistance; Ann Moore for her exceptional secretarial skills; Heather Jones, my friend and partner in Clevedon Country Catering; Gail Condor and Penny Fallaver, Betty Nash, Ann and Drew Hayward, the Chitty family and Keith Kelly for their special help with locations; and my fishing friends Cliff Fenwick, Peter and Stella Gordon (The Store, Te Rangi-ita), Greg and Deb Hurt and Father Jude McCarthy. Last but not least, thank you to Ross, Katie and Guy Seagar for your love and patience.

The following Auckland people and organisations are gratefully acknowledged for their help:
Michael Brajkovich, Clevedon Country Market, Southern Fresh Produce Ltd (Pukekohe), Clevedon Antiques and Collectibles, Victoriana Antiques and Curios, Kesaria, Studio Ceramics, Fionna Hill, Gilbert Powerie and Co Ltd, Indigo, and The Family Barrow (all of Parnell), Seaside Meats (Beachlands), Rainbow Yacht Charters (Westhaven), Lord Ponsonby's Delicatessen (Ponsonby), Andrew and Jeannie van der Putten and Ray James Ltd (Grey Lynn), Casa (St Lukes), Italian Ceramics Ltd (Three Kings), Living & Giving (Mt Eden) Palmers Garden World (Newmarket) and CS Agencies.

# CONTENTS

# INTRODUCTION

No matter what the different ethnic and cultural influences have been over the last years, New Zealand country cuisine has now come of age. I have wanted to write a cookbook to acknowledge this fact for some time and, now that it is completed at last, it is my great pleasure to invite you to share this celebration of the unique pleasures of New Zealand country cooking.

We are so fortunate to live in a country where the environment is fresh and clean so that our local produce and other brilliant raw ingredients remain free from pollution. I've been lucky enough to drink champagne, eat caviar and many other exotic dishes in some of the world's most glamorous surroundings. These experiences have taught me to shed many culinary inhibitions but for me home is best — the place where I want to be, where the quality of fresh ingredients remains unrivalled and where I grew up learning that cooking good food for family and friends is one of life's greatest pleasures. I always maintain that just because a meal is incredibly complicated to prepare and cook doesn't mean that it will necessarily be incredibly successful. Great food does, of course, involve some work but I like to give my guests that subtle illusion of effortlessness which is so conducive to a relaxed and enjoyable gathering. Relying on uncomplicated cooking methods and excellent local ingredients is my main secret for a successful meal.

My culinary education started with my mother who was my greatest teacher. I grew up with a real interest and love for cooking which, in later years, was greatly influenced by some of the world's finest cooks including Julia Child and Keith Floyd. It was these experts who taught me about style, technique and, perhaps most importantly, gusto.

Cooking courses both here and overseas have furthered my culinary knowledge and for some years now I've been writing a regular food column and running my own cooking courses. It's truly a marvellous thing when your passion can also be your profession and I continue to relish the opportunity to share the secrets of good food.

In preparing this collection of recipes I've had enormous fun mixing old and new with what some might call happy abandonment. An important factor for me was the re-creation of a number of recipes to remind me of the country flavours and themes that I grew up with so happily. I wanted this book to convey as much about the joys of sharing good food with family and friends as about the art of country cooking itself. And if I had to confine my cooking philosophy to just a few words it could be boiled down, no pun intended, to simple, uncomplicated cooking methods that take best advantage of excellent fresh ingredients.

Jo Seagar

*'The pleasures of the table — that lovely old-fashioned phrase — depict food as an art form, as a delightful part of civilised life. In spite of food fads, fitness programs and health concerns, we must never lose sight of a beautifully conceived meal.'*

*JULIA CHILD*

# BREAKFASTS AND BRUNCHES

*Family breakfasts during the week are a thing of the past for many of us. These days it's everyone for themselves and watching the television advertisements, portraying families sitting around a pine table with all the time in the world, is the closest we ever get to this idyllic scene.*

*Yet it's worth making time for a special breakfast or brunch. It can be enormous fun and encourages a feeling of absolute luxury when you and your family or guests start the morning in such a wonderful way. Preparing and indulging in a meal at this time of day, when there's time to relax and enjoy the food and the surroundings, is close to the top of my list of favourite ways to entertain. And it's wonderful to live in a country where there's so much scope for eating outside: there's something inherently cosy about brunch whether it's outdoors or indoors.*

*Breakfasts and brunches offer the opportunity to combine sweet and savoury dishes in a different order to other meals — you can start with fruit and finish with something savoury. Here, then, is my favourite collection.*

# T O A S T E D   C H E E S E   M U F F I N S

*This is my basic muffin recipe. I love to make muffins at the drop of a hat and it's fun to experiment with different varieties. I particularly like fruity ones, made with feijoas and persimmons.*

*The secret to success is in not overworking the mixture — just a light binding of ingredients, keeping the mixture runny and wet. Use non-stick, deep muffin tins. I hardly ever wash my tins, just a wipe with paper towels or a damp cloth is all the care they need.*

2 cups flour
4 teaspoons baking powder
½ teaspoon salt
1 cup grated tasty cheese
1 egg
¼ cup oil
1¼ cups milk

Stir all ingredients together in a large bowl, just lightly mixing to combine. Don't overwork the mixture or the muffins will be tough and heavy.

Spoon the mixture, which should be fairly runny and pourable, into deep non-stick muffin tins. Sprinkle a few shreds of grated cheese over. Bake in a hot oven for 15–20 minutes until golden brown.

### Variations:

To make savoury muffins, add any of the following to the Toasted Cheese Muffin recipe: chopped herbs, finely sliced spring onions, nuts, a tablespoon of fruit chutney or relish, chopped pickled onions or gherkins, crumbled blue cheese, chopped ginger or crushed garlic.

**Makes 12**

# F R E S H   S T R A W B E R R Y   A N D   C I N N A M O N   M U F F I N S

2 cups flour
4 teaspoons baking powder
1 egg
¼ cup oil
1¼ cups milk
½ cup sugar
1 cup fresh strawberries, hulled and diced
1 teaspoon cinnamon
extra sugar to taste

Stir all ingredients together in a large bowl, just lightly mixing to combine. Taste for sweetness and add extra sugar if required. The mixture should be runny and pourable. Spoon into deep non-stick muffin tins. Bake in a hot oven for 15–20 minutes until golden brown.

**Makes 12**

# COFFEE MAPLE WALNUT MUFFINS

2 tablespoons instant coffee powder
¼ cup milk
2½ cups flour
4 teaspoons baking powder
1 egg
¼ cup oil
1¼ cups milk
½ cup sugar
¾ cup chopped walnuts
2 tablespoons maple syrup

Dissolve instant coffee powder in the milk. Stir all ingredients together in a large bowl, just lightly mixing to combine. Taste for sweetness and add extra sugar if required. The mixture should be runny and pourable. Spoon into deep non-stick muffin tins. Bake in a hot oven for 15–20 minutes until golden brown.

**Makes 12**

# FRESH PEACH AND HONEY MUFFINS

2 cups flour
4 teaspoons baking powder
1 egg
¼ cup oil
1¼ cups milk
½ cup sugar
1 cup peaches, peeled and finely chopped
½ teaspoon mixed spice
2 tablespoons liquid honey
extra sugar to taste

Warm honey. Stir all ingredients together in a large bowl, just lightly mixing to combine. Taste for sweetness and add extra sugar if required. The mixture should be runny and pourable. Spoon into deep non-stick muffin tins. Bake in a hot oven for 15–20 minutes until golden brown.

**Makes 12**

# MORNING GLORY MUFFINS

2 cups flour
4 teaspoons baking powder
1 egg
¼ cup oil
1¼–1¾ cups milk
½ cup grated carrot
½ cup sultanas
½ cup grated apple
1 tablespoon desiccated coconut

Stir all ingredients together in a large bowl, just lightly mixing to combine. Extra milk may be necessary to achieve a runny, pourable mixture. Spoon into deep non-stick muffin tins. Bake in a hot oven for 15–20 minutes until golden brown.

**Makes 12**

## Peanut Butter Sultana Muffins

*2 cups flour*
*4 teaspoons baking powder*
*1 egg*
*¼ cup oil*
*1¼ cups milk*
*½ cup sugar*
*4 tablespoons crunchy peanut butter*
*½ cup sultanas*
*extra sugar to taste*

Stir all ingredients together in a large bowl, just lightly mixing to combine. Taste for sweetness and add extra sugar if required. The mixture should be runny and pourable. Spoon into deep non-stick muffin tins. Bake in a hot oven for 15–20 minutes until golden brown.

**Makes 12**

## Rhubarb Sour Cream And Cinnamon Muffins

*2 ½ cups flour*
*4 teaspoons baking powder*
*2 teaspoons ground cinnamon*
*1 egg*
*¼ cup oil*
*1¼ cups milk*
*½ cup sugar*
*1 cup stewed rhubarb*
*½ cup sour cream*
*extra sugar to taste*

Stir all ingredients together in a large bowl, just lightly mixing to combine. Taste for sweetness and add extra sugar if required. The mixture should be runny and pourable. Spoon into deep non-stick muffin tins. Bake in a hot oven for 15–20 minutes until golden brown.

**Makes 12**

*Muffins are incredibly versatile and lend themselves well to different combinations of flavours and textures such as the* **PEANUT BUTTER SULTANA MUFFINS** *pictured here. Let your imagination run wild in coming up with your own flavour combinations.*

# WAFFLES

In our family, brunch means waffles. I just can't seem to get away with anything else for this meal. Sometimes I serve them with crispy oven-cooked bacon, maple syrup, bananas and cream. And other times I make them a base for poached or scrambled eggs and grilled tomatoes. They are also wonderful served with raspberries or strawberries with cream.

250 g self-raising flour
2 tablespoons castor sugar
3 eggs, separated
1½ cups milk
100 g butter, melted
1 teaspoon vanilla
extra butter for greasing waffle iron

Sift flour and sugar into a bowl. Mix in egg yolks, milk, melted butter and vanilla. Mix to a smooth batter. In a separate bowl beat egg whites until stiff peaks form, then fold carefully into the batter.

Brush a heated waffle iron with melted butter, spoon in 2–3 tablespoons of batter and cook until the waffles are crisp and golden brown. Serve warm with whipped cream and maple syrup.

### Variation:

Add ½ teaspoon mixed spice to the batter and serve with poached apple slices and cinnamon cream or honey.

### Makes 8

Who's for brunch? **BREAKFAST PANCAKES** with maple syrup, fresh fruit and pecan nuts (page 16) or **WAFFLES** with blueberries and whipped cream will have them queuing up.

## BREAKFAST PANCAKES

*2 eggs*
*1 cup milk approximately*
*1½ cups self-raising flour*
*2–3 tablespoons sugar*

Use a food processor or electric beater to mix all the ingredients together quickly until smooth.

Grease a heavy frypan or use a non-stick crêpe pan. Drop tablespoonfuls of mixture into the preheated pan and cook over a medium heat until golden brown on the underside. Turn over and cook on the other side.

Stack the pancakes on a plate as they come out of the pan and keep the pile covered with a clean tea towel so that the pancakes stay soft.

Serve with maple or golden syrup, whipped cream, fresh fruit (bananas and berries are particularly good), or with stewed or canned fruit.

### Variations:

Changing the basic theme is easy. Just add approximately ½ cup raw fruit such as blueberries or apples to the mixture after mixing. For spicy sweet pancakes, add ½ teaspoon cinnamon and a pinch of cloves plus 2 tablespoons of liquid honey to the mixture. Or replace ½ cup self-raising flour with ½ cup oatmeal, cornmeal, whole wheat flour or rolled oats.

### Makes about 6–8 pancakes

## APRICOT LOAF

*This makes marvellous 'special' toast for brunch and it's also nice served fresh, in thin buttered slices topped with cheese.*

*1 cup dried apricots, chopped*
*1 cup boiling water*
*2 eggs*
*1 cup sugar*
*50 g butter, melted*
*1 cup chopped walnuts*
*2¾ cups flour*
*1 teaspoon baking powder*
*½ teaspoon soda*
*½ teaspoon salt*

Soak dried apricots in the boiling water for 20 minutes. Beat eggs and sugar until creamy, add melted butter, apricots and water and mix in walnuts and dry ingredients. Mix well. Spoon into a well-greased loaf tin and bake at 160°C for 1¼ hours. Cool on a wire rack and slice when cold.

# CRISPY POTATO CAKES

*After a zillion attempts, variations and dissections of American brunch restaurant versions of hash browns and potato cakes, I think this is the best way to make these crispy potato cakes.*
*For a very special brunch, try these topped with oysters or smoked salmon, sour cream and caviar — heaven in a mouthful.*

10–12 large potatoes
a little oil for cooking
salt and pepper
optional extras (see Method)

Peel the potatoes and steam them until they are just soft. When they are cool enough to handle, grate them either by hand or with a grater blade in the food processor.

Heat a large, preferably non-stick frypan, until hot. Pour in a little oil, then spoon in a good handful-size of grated potato, flatten with a spatula and sprinkle generously with salt and pepper. All sorts of optional bits and pieces may be added at this stage. Finely sliced spring onion or finely chopped onion, cooked bacon bits, diced ham, grated cheese, chopped herbs, chive flowers, paprika, chilli or finely chopped red and green capsicum (great for a festive Christmas brunch). Another spoonful of grated potato over the extras will enclose the filling.

Press down firmly with the spatula, then after 3–4 minutes when the edges are showing crispy and golden, turn over and cook on the other side. Keep warm, uncovered in the oven, until you've cooked the whole batch, and serve immediately.

**Makes about 8–10**

# BAKED EGGS WITH BRIE CHEESE

*I always cook eggs this way when doing them for a crowd.*

Per portion:
30 g slice Brie cheese
1 egg
1 tablespoon cream
salt and freshly ground black pepper to taste
finely chopped parsley to garnish

Preheat oven to 180°C. Press slices of Brie into the base of the required number of well-buttered individual small ramekin dishes. Break egg into each ramekin over the Brie, then spoon the cream over. Generously dust with pepper and add salt to taste. Place ramekins in a roasting pan and pour hot water into the pan to come three-quarters of the way up the sides of the ramekins. Bake for approximately 15–20 minutes, depending on how well set you prefer your eggs. Sprinkle with parsley and serve immediately.

*On a clear crisp winter's day wrap up warmly and get ready for a piping hot **SUNDAY BRUNCH FRITTATA** pictured left.*

# SUNDAY BRUNCH FRITTATA

*Frittatas are wonderful, served hot for brunch, but they also taste great when cold. Make them for picnic lunches when you want something hearty and substantial but don't have time to make a pie.*

2 tablespoons oil

50 g butter

2 medium-sized onions, finely chopped

3 cloves garlic, crushed

5 medium-sized cold, cooked red potatoes, cooked in their skins, sliced

1 small red capsicum, seeded and finely chopped

1 small green capsicum, seeded and finely chopped

1 cup sliced button mushrooms

2 tablespoons chopped fresh herbs (parsley, chives, basil etc.)

salt and pepper

8 large eggs

¼ cup milk or cream

2 cups grated tasty cheese

Heat the oil and butter in a large, preferably non-stick, frypan. Add the onions and garlic and cook until softened. Add potatoes, peppers and mushrooms and cook for a few minutes. Stir in the chopped herbs and season to taste.

Beat the eggs and cream together and stir in half of the grated cheese. Pour the egg mixture over the vegetables and shake the pan gently so that the egg settles evenly. Cook over a gentle heat to set the sides and bottom.

Remove pan from heat, sprinkle the top of the frittata with the remaining cheese and brown under the grill. Cut into wedges and serve immediately.

***Serves 4–6***

# EGGS BAKED IN BREAD ROLLS WITH PESTO HOLLANDAISE

6 round bread rolls
50 g butter
3 medium-sized onions, finely sliced
200 g grated tasty cheese
salt and freshly ground black pepper
6 large eggs
basil leaves to garnish

Cut a slice from the top of each bread roll. Scoop out most of the doughy centre and discard, leaving a shell about 1 cm thick.

Melt the butter in a large frypan, add the sliced onion and cook over a gentle heat until softened. Place bread roll shells into a baking dish and spoon some cooked onion into each. Top with grated cheese. Season to taste then carefully break an egg into each roll. Bake in a hot oven, 200°C, for 10–12 minutes until the whites are just firm and the yolks still soft.

Before serving, ladle a spoonful of Pesto Hollandaise over each roll and garnish with fresh basil leaves. Serve immediately.

## PESTO HOLLANDAISE

3 egg yolks
1 tablespoon lemon juice
1 tablespoon white wine vinegar
250 g butter
1 teaspoon pesto sauce or substitute
   1 tablespoon fresh chopped basil leaves
freshly ground black pepper

In a food processor or blender mix the egg yolks, lemon juice and white wine vinegar. Melt the butter, either in a microwave or a small saucepan, and, keeping the food processor running, pour the melted butter into the egg yolk mixture. Add the pesto or chopped basil leaves and process briefly. Season to taste and serve immediately, while still warm.

**Serves 6**

**EGGS BAKED IN BREAD ROLLS WITH PESTO HOLLANDAISE** is a tasty and easy variation on bacon and eggs. The Pesto Hollandaise adds a touch of sophistication to these traditional ingredients, making it an ideal dish to serve when you have special guests. Use chunks of olive bread or French bread for a change and you can also replace the pesto sauce or basil in the Hollandaise Sauce with any herb or spice to give it your own special touch.

# SPINACH CRÊPES WITH BLUE CHEESE AND BUTTON MUSHROOMS

1 cup flour
4 eggs
1 teaspoon salt
generous amount of freshly ground black
    pepper
1½ cups milk
2 tablespoons oil
½ cup cooked chopped spinach, well drained
sour cream and extra blue vein cheese to
    garnish

Mix all the ingredients except sour cream and extra cheese in a food processor or blender. Heat a small non-stick crêpe pan or a well-oiled frypan over a medium-high heat. Pour in a ladleful of batter and tilt the pan so that the mixture evenly covers the bottom in a thin film. When the batter no longer looks wet in the centre, ease the edges of the crêpe away from the sides of the frypan. Carefully turn the crêpe and briefly cook the other side. Remove crêpe from pan and repeat cooking procedure until all batter is used.

Stack cooked crêpes and keep them covered with a clean tea towel to prevent them from drying out.

## FILLING

100 g blue vein cheese, crumbled
1 cup sliced button mushrooms
freshly ground black pepper to taste

Place a spoonful of cheese, topped with sliced mushrooms, in the centre of each crêpe. Roll up in the traditional way or fold over the sides to make small packages. Place crêpes on a lightly buttered baking tray and cook until warmed through. Serve with sour cream sprinkled with a little extra crumbled blue vein cheese.

**Makes 12–15 crêpes**

# FRESH PINEAPPLE AND BANANAS WRAPPED IN BACON

*These make ideal accompaniments to poached eggs, crispy potato cakes, omelettes or waffles.*

1 medium-sized pineapple
6 bananas
12 rashers bacon, lightly cooked

Peel and cut up the pineapple into six wedges and peel the bananas. Wrap each piece of fruit (the bananas should be left whole) in the precooked rashers and secure with toothpicks. Grill on both sides to finish the crisping process. Remove toothpicks and serve immediately.

**Serves 6**

# PRAWN AND AVOCADO SOUFFLÉS

*The coolness of avocado flesh and prawns combined with this hot cheesy soufflé topping is a fabulous taste sensation.*

3 firm, ripe avocados
½ cup cooked small prawns or shrimps
juice of 1 small lemon
50 g butter
1 tablespoon flour
salt and pepper
1 cup milk
2 eggs, separated
1 cup grated tasty cheese

Cut the avocados in half and remove stones. Make a small slice across the base of each half so they sit flat, cut side up. Evenly divide the prawns between each half, filling the hollows left by the stones. Sprinkle prawns with lemon juice.

Melt the butter in a small saucepan. Add the flour, salt and pepper. Gradually add the milk, whisking constantly until the sauce thickens. Whisk in the egg yolks and grated cheese. Stir until sauce is smooth and well combined. In a bowl beat the egg whites until stiff and carefully fold into the sauce. Place avocados on a grill tray and spoon sauce over so that the top of each is completely covered. Place under a hot grill and cook until they are puffy and golden, about 3–4 minutes. Don't cook them for too long as the avocado flesh will turn bitter. Serve immediately garnished with fresh herbs.

# ASPARAGUS TIP OMELETTE WITH FRESH TARRAGON

10–12 asparagus spears
5 large eggs
2 tablespoons cream
50 g butter
salt and freshly ground black pepper
1 teaspoon finely chopped fresh tarragon

Cut or snap tips from the asparagus spears and cook them in boiling water until just tender. Drain well and refresh under cold running water.

Break the eggs into a large bowl and add the cream. Beat with a whisk until yolks, whites and cream are well blended. Melt the butter in a frypan over a high heat and when foaming, tilt the pan to evenly coat the surface. Pour in beaten egg and cook until the omelette is golden brown underneath and set. Turn heat down and place asparagus tips across half of the omelette's surface. Sprinkle with the chopped tarragon and salt and pepper. Gently fold the other half of the omelette over the asparagus. Cut in half while still in the pan and slide on to two serving plates. Serve with triangles of whole-grain toast and butter.

**Serves 2**

# FIRST COURSES AND LUNCHEONS

*While I've called this chapter First Courses and Luncheons, it is not necessarily restricted to this as it covers a variety of small dishes which can be eaten at any meal. And think about serving several at once in the style of restaurant eating, when you choose several entrées rather than committing yourself to just one main course dish. This style of eating allows you to combine different tastes and flavours and it works just as well for home entertaining.*

*There's plenty of room for experimenting, too. Gone are the days when there were rigid rules in force governing the serving of food, dictating the precise number of courses, their order and how to serve them — that's all outmoded now. As long as you and your guests feel comfortable about it, there can't be any such thing as the right or wrong way.*

*When entertaining, lunch is the ideal meal for serving several light dishes. Let the seasons and your own instinct for combining colours, tastes and textures be your guide. And if time allows you to prepare only one dish, the addition of salad, bread, fruit and cheese will always stretch a meal with style.*

# CREAMY CAULIFLOWER AND CHEESE CHOWDER

*1 small cauliflower, cut in florets, retain stem*
*2 cups chicken stock*
*1 bay leaf*
*salt and freshly ground black pepper*
*1 medium-sized onion, sliced*
*50 g butter*
*2 tablespoons flour*
*¾ cup milk*
*100 g tasty Cheddar cheese, grated*
*cream and fresh herbs to garnish*

Chop stem of cauliflower into small pieces and place, with florets, in stock. Add bay leaf, salt and pepper and onion. Simmer for 20 minutes until tender. Remove bay leaf and blend in a food processor until smooth.

Melt butter in a large saucepan over a medium heat. Whisk in flour, cook for a couple of minutes, then stir in the milk. Keep whisking and add purée, stirring all the time over a gentle heat. Stir in grated cheese. Check seasoning, making sure it's good and peppery. Add a little cream if desired. Serve in warm soup bowls with snipped herbs such as chive flowers and crispy croutons.

### Variation:

Interesting crouton flavours, such as crispy Parmesan, garlic, chilli, or thyme, can really add that final clever touch to a soup. I simply panfry cubes or chunks of bread in a mixture of oil and butter and sprinkle with the flavour I feel like using at the time.

***Serves 6***

# CHESTNUT AND SHERRY SOUP

*If you want to make this soup for a festive occasion, such as Christmas dinner, make croutons in shapes to suit the occasion, e.g. little Christmas trees, to float on top.*

*125 g butter*
*2 large onions, roughly chopped*
*1 large carrot, roughly chopped*
*1 parsnip, roughly chopped*
*1 cup chopped celery*
*1 large potato, peeled and roughly chopped*
*6 cups chicken stock*
*1 cup medium-to-dry sherry*
*3 tablespoons finely grated nutmeg*
*300 g can unsweetened chestnut purée*
*2 cups cream*
*paprika or finely chopped herbs to garnish*

Melt butter in a large saucepan. Add onion and soften for 2 minutes over a medium heat. Add all other ingredients except for cream. Bring to the boil then reduce heat and simmer for 30 minutes. Purée the soup in batches, in a blender or food processor, and pass through a sieve to extract any lumpy bits or celery fibre.

Transfer to a clean heavy-based saucepan, stir in the cream and simmer gently to heat up. Ladle into soup plates and serve with a swirl of cream and a sprinkling of paprika or finely chopped herbs to garnish.

***Serves 6***

# KUMARA AND CHILLI SOUP

60 g butter
1 large onion, roughly chopped
1 clove of garlic, crushed
5 medium-sized kumaras, peeled and diced
4 cups chicken or good quality vegetable stock
sweet chilli sauce or minced fresh chilli pepper
½ teaspoon cinnamon
1 cup cream
salt and freshly ground black pepper
1–2 tablespoons chopped parsley to garnish

Melt butter in a large saucepan, add onion and garlic and cook until soft, about 2–3 minutes. Add kumara and stock. Cover saucepan and simmer for 15–20 minutes, until kumara is soft.

Purée mixture in a blender or food processor and return to saucepan. Stir in the chilli, cinnamon and cream. Gently reheat and season to taste with salt and pepper. Garnish with chopped parsley and, if desired, croutons. Crispy wholemeal ones with a dusting of paprika look and taste particularly nice with this soup.

**Serves 4–6**

# FIELD MUSHROOM SOUP WITH FRESH THYME

*If field mushrooms are not available, substitute cultivated ones.*

250 g field mushrooms
75 g butter
2 cloves garlic, crushed
1 medium-sized onion, chopped
2 tablespoons flour
1 teaspoon chopped fresh thyme or lemon
    thyme
2½ cups chicken stock or milk
salt
1 teaspoon lemon pepper seasoning or freshly
    ground black pepper
150 g sour cream
grated cheese and chopped thyme or parsley
    to garnish

Slice mushrooms, trimming away any tough ends from stalks. Melt butter in a large saucepan, add garlic and onion and cook for 5–6 minutes until soft. Add mushrooms, stir, and cook over a medium heat for 5 minutes. Add flour and thyme, stir through then add stock or milk and salt and lemon pepper. Bring to the boil then reduce heat and simmer for 15 minutes. Stir in sour cream, reserving a little for garnish. Adjust seasoning. Serve garnished with extra sour cream, a sprinkling of grated cheese and fresh herbs.

### Variations:

This soup can be puréed in a blender or food processor for a thick creamy version. Adding crumbled blue cheese also makes it rather special for a dinner party. In this case, garnish with crumbled blue cheese and slices of fresh mushrooms.

**Serves 4–6**

# CREAMY SMOKED SEAFOOD CHOWDER

*This recipe can be the base for adding any sort of seafood. Lots of smoked varieties are particularly good as they have such great flavour.*

6 rashers streaky bacon, finely chopped
100 g butter
2 large onions, peeled and chopped
3 tablespoons flour
4 cups milk
4 cups Fish Stock (see recipe following)
310 g can smoked fish fillets
3 large potatoes, peeled and diced
400 g can cream-style sweetcorn
2 cups assorted seafood (shrimps, surimi,
    pipis, tuatuas, smoked mussels, sliced fresh
    or smoked fish fillets)
2 teaspoons dried thyme
salt and freshly ground black pepper to taste
2 tablespoons coarsely chopped parsley to
    garnish
1 cup of cream optional

Fry bacon in a large stockpot until crisp. Remove and place on paper towels to drain. Add the butter to the bacon fat in the stockpot over a medium heat. Add the chopped onion and cook until soft. Stir in the flour and while stirring with a wire whisk, gradually blend in the milk, followed by the fish stock. Add smoked fish fillets including the liquid. Add the diced potato, sweetcorn, mixed seafood, thyme, bacon and salt and pepper.

Simmer over a very gentle heat, stirring regularly, for about 30 minutes until the diced potato is well cooked and the soup is smooth and creamy. Stir in the cream just before serving and garnish with parsley (or some fresh dill or chives).

### Variation:

Make the soup as directed up to adding the cream and garnishing. Chill the soup and, when quite cold, ladle into individual soup bowls. Roll out rounds of flaky pastry (or cut out from pre-rolled pastry sheets). Carefully secure the pastry lids on to the bowls, sticking the pastry down with water. Use pastry scraps to decorate each serving, cut out little fish shapes, leaves etc., and secure these by brushing with water and pressing on firmly. Brush each lid with an egg wash (1 tablespoon water mixed with 1 egg yolk) and bake in a hot oven, 200°C, for about 20–25 minutes, until the pastry is puffed and golden and the soup piping hot.

*Serves 6 hearty bowls full*

## FISH STOCK

1 kg fish heads, bones and trimmings,
    crayfish shells, or any white fish such as
    snapper, tarakihi, chopped
1 onion, roughly chopped
12 parsley stems
2 tablespoons fresh lemon juice
½ teaspoon salt
3¾ cups cold water
½ cup dry white wine

In a heavy saucepan combine the fish bones and trimmings, onion, parsley, lemon juice, and salt and steam the mixture, covered, over a moderately high heat for 5 minutes. Add water and the wine. Bring the liquid to the boil, skim the froth, and cook the stock over a moderate heat for 30 minutes. Strain the stock through a fine sieve into a bowl, pressing hard on the solids, and let it cool. The stock may then be frozen. This recipe makes a good concentrated fish stock.

*Makes 4 cups*

**BLOODY MARY SOUP** *pictured above, is a refreshing addition to an outdoor meal. Make it up at home and transport it to your destination in a thermos to keep it icy cold.*

*Right:* **CREAMY SMOKED SEAFOOD CHOWDER,** *served in generous portions, is a fabulous meal in itself. It's one of my favourite recipes because you can toss in any seafood that you might have on hand.*

# BLOODY MARY SOUP

*3 cups tomato juice*
*2×400 g cans peeled whole tomatoes in juice*
*1 cup vodka*
*crushed ice*
*½ teaspoon freshly ground black pepper*
*3 tablespoons fresh mint leaves, finely*
  *chopped*
*1 teaspoon Worcestershire sauce*
*1 spring onion, finely chopped*
*salt to taste*
*fresh herbs and celery to garnish*

Blend all ingredients thoroughly in a blender or food processor and serve in tall glasses or glass mugs. Garnish with fresh snipped herbs, parsley and mint, etc. and a stalk of celery.

**Serves 4–6**

## AUTUMN PUMPKIN AND CINNAMON SOUP

*1 medium-sized pumpkin, peeled and roughly*
  *diced*
*1 large onion, chopped*
*2 cloves of garlic, crushed*
*200 g butter*
*1 teaspoon cinnamon*
*a little milk*
*1¼ cups cream*
*salt and freshly ground black pepper*
*chopped parsley and yoghurt or cream to*
  *garnish*

Just cover the pumpkin, onion and garlic with water and cook over a medium heat until the pumpkin is very soft and the water has mostly evaporated. Allow to cool slightly, then purée in a blender or food processor in batches, adding the butter and cinnamon with a little milk to thin the mixture if required. Return to the saucepan and stir in the cream and season with salt and pepper. Reheat gently, and serve garnished with chopped parsley and a swirl of yoghurt or cream.

**Serves 6**

## GREEK-STYLE CHICKEN AND LEMON SOUP

*I often enhance home-made stock with some canned or tetrapak stock or chicken consommé. In fact this is a great soup to make with bought stock and a portion of rotisserie chicken picked up on the way home from work. When buying stock or canned soups and broths, it pays to read the labels of all the various brands and choose the one with the fewest unpronounceable chemical names, and the lowest sodium content.*

*12 cups well-flavoured chicken stock*
*1 cup long grain rice*
*1–2 cups shredded chicken meat*
*3 eggs*
*grated zest and juice of 3 large lemons*
*salt and freshly ground pepper*
*1 tablespoon chopped parsley*

Bring the stock to the boil then add the rice and chicken meat. Stir until it boils again, then simmer for 12–15 minutes until the rice is well cooked.

In a small bowl whisk together the eggs, lemon zest and juice. While whisking, gradually add a cup of the hot chicken broth.

Stir this mixture into the chicken soup. Season to taste and add parsley. Serve immediately. Do not reheat this soup after the egg mixture has been added because the egg curdles and turns into ribbons of scrambled egg.

To make this soup more of a meal, add more chicken and a few green vegetables such as diced zucchini, beans, etc. Served with crusty bread and cheese it would be extremely filling and satisfying.

**Serves 4–6**

# CHILLED AVOCADO, LIME AND WATERCRESS SOUP

*As this is a very rich, creamy soup, serve in smaller portions. It looks particularly attractive served in small glass dessert or parfait dishes.*

1 medium-sized onion, finely chopped
1 clove garlic, crushed
50 g butter
1 bunch watercress, roughly chopped
2 cups chicken stock
4 large ripe avocados, peeled, pitted and
    roughly chopped
150 g sour cream
grated zest and juice of 4 limes
salt and freshly ground black pepper
1 lime, thinly sliced

In a large saucepan gently fry onion and garlic in butter until soft. Add watercress, reserving a little for garnish, and stock. Bring to the boil, then simmer for 15 minutes. Purée in a blender or food processor, then push through a sieve. Chill.

Purée avocados and add to chilled broth together with sour cream (reserving a little for garnish), lime juice and lime zest. Before adding salt and pepper, taste the soup as the watercress is quite peppery. Garnish with a swirl of sour cream and lime slices, with a sprig of watercress.

**Variation:**

Natural yoghurt can be substituted for sour cream.

**Serves 4–6**

# CREAMY BLUE CHEESE AND APPLE SOUP

1 small onion, finely chopped
1 stalk of celery, chopped
4 apples, peeled, cored and sliced
60 g butter
4 cups chicken stock
200 g blue cheese
1 cup cream
1 cup white wine
¼ teaspoon ground nutmeg
salt and freshly ground black pepper to taste
parsley sprigs, sliced apple and plain yoghurt
    to garnish

Gently fry onion, celery and apple in the butter in a large saucepan until soft. Add chicken stock and simmer for 20 minutes. Cool slightly and purée with blue cheese in a blender or food processor. Return mixture to the saucepan, add cream, wine, nutmeg, salt and pepper to taste, and reheat. Garnish with parsley sprigs, slices of apple or a swirl of yoghurt.

**Serves 4–6**

*Not only does* **AVOCADO WITH SMOKED SALMON AND CAVIAR** *look really good but the flavours and textures taste wonderful, too.*

# AVOCADO WITH SMOKED SALMON AND CAVIAR

*An impressive entrée presentation which is very easy to prepare. It's a good vehicle for offering just a little portion of seafood for each guest based on the loaves and fishes principle.*

*3 avocados, firm but ripe*
*alfalfa sprouts*
*150 g tub sour cream*
*50–100 g smoked salmon, thinly sliced*
*3 teaspoons caviar or salmon roe*
*sprigs of dill or other fresh herbs*
*Classic Vinaigrette Dressing*

Slice avocados in half lengthways. Remove and discard stones. Sit each avocado half on a bed of alfalfa sprouts. Spoon a little sour cream into the stone cavity then garnish with a swirl of smoked salmon and a dollop of caviar. Add herb sprigs of your choice and serve with a little Classic Vinaigrette Dressing to the side.

### Variations:

All sorts of variations are possible using different salad leaves or sprouts as the base. Different seafoods, such as shrimps, crayfish meat or smoked fish, can also be used for the filling and different herbs and garnishes.

## WHITEBAIT

*I was so disappointed when I ordered whitebait in an English restaurant and expected the minute, thread-like transparent little fishies we know and love in New Zealand. Along came a plate of perfectly cooked, perfectly okay small, sprat-like fishes. They tasted great, but they just weren't anything like our own beloved version.*

*These days whitebait is a real delicacy. Where I now have to speak in terms of 100 grams, my father talks of whole 'kerosene' drums of the stuff in the South Island in his youth and even I remember catching buckets full in my net with my Aunty Betty, knee-deep in the Waikanae River north of Wellington.*

*Whitebait fritters are by far the best and most popular way to serve this tiny but esteemed fish. The batter should be a very light egg mixture, just holding the threads together. They shouldn't be at all floury and it's better to have fewer fritters crammed absolutely full of whitebait, than to try to stretch them with more egg mixture.*

# WHITEBAIT FRITTERS

1 heaped tablespoon flour
2 eggs, beaten
½ teaspoon salt
freshly ground black pepper
250 g whitebait
butter or a mixture of butter and oil for
   frying

Mix flour, eggs, salt and pepper to a smooth batter and fold in the whitebait. Heat a large frypan over a medium heat. Add butter and, when bubbling, ladle in spoonfuls of batter. Cook for approximately 2 minutes on each side and serve immediately with juicy lemon or lime wedges.

**Makes about 12 fritters**

## SHELLFISH FRITTERS

*1 egg, lightly beaten*
*1 cup self-raising flour*
*½ teaspoon salt and freshly ground black*
 *pepper*
*1 tablespoon finely chopped parsley (optional)*
*milk to mix*
*1 cup shellfish meat, chopped or minced*
*butter and oil for frying*

Mix egg, flour, salt and pepper, parsley and sufficient milk to make a creamy batter. Fold the shellfish into the batter. Heat a large frypan over a medium heat. Add butter and oil and when bubbling, ladle in dessertspoonfuls of batter. Cook for 2–3 minutes on each side until golden brown. Use a mix of butter and oil for frying. Drain on paper towels and eat immediately with lemon wedges for squeezing over fresh juice.

**Makes about 12 fritters**

## OYSTERS

*I thank my lucky stars that the gods didn't keep Bluff oysters to themselves. I've tried oysters all over the globe, but nothing compares with my favourite plump, juicy Bluff oysters from the cold, clean southern waters of New Zealand. Eaten raw with brown bread and butter, a dusting of freshly ground black pepper and a squeeze of lemon juice, they are superb.*

## PACIFIC OYSTERS WITH WINE MIGNONETTE

*2 dozen oysters in the shell, scrubbed*
*1 spring onion*
*¼ cup red wine vinegar*
*¼ cup sparkling wine or champagne*
*freshly ground black pepper*

Open oysters and place them, in their bottom shells, on serving plates. Chop the white part of the spring onion very finely and reserve the green end for another recipe. In a small bowl mix the remaining ingredients, including the spring onion, to make the mignonette sauce. Let diners dip their oysters into the sauce or serve little individual dishes of the sauce in scooped-out lemon halves.

**Serves 4**

# POLYNESIAN-STYLE MARINATED FISH

600 g fresh, firm white fish fillets
½ cup fresh lemon or lime juice
400 ml can coconut cream
salt and freshly ground black pepper
2 teaspoons finely shredded lemon peel
2 tablespoons finely diced red capsicum
3 tablespoons coarsely chopped parsley
1 tablespoon finely chopped fresh coriander or
    fresh dill
3 passionfruit
1 cup fresh or canned pineapple pieces
1 pawpaw
4 kiwifruit
4 firm but ripe bananas
sprigs of dill, coriander and parsley to garnish

Remove any skin and bones from the fish and cut into thin finger-like strips. Toss with the lemon juice and allow to marinate, covered, in the refrigerator for 3–4 hours or overnight.

Just before serving, drain the fish and squeeze gently to remove most of the lemon juice. Toss with sufficient coconut cream to coat, and season with salt and pepper. Mix in the lemon shreds, diced capsicum, parsley and herbs.

Cut the passionfruit in halves, peel and slice the other fruits and arrange with the fish on serving plates, garnished with the fresh herbs.

**Serves 6–8**

# BLINIS

2 cups flour
1 cup buckwheat flour
1 teaspoon salt
2 teaspoons active dry yeast granules
1¼ cups warm milk
3 eggs, separated
300 ml cream, lightly whipped

Mix flour, buckwheat flour, salt and yeast. Add warm milk mixed with beaten egg yolks. Mix to a smooth batter. Cover with cling film and allow to stand in a warm place for an hour or so until frothy.

Fold lightly whipped cream and stiffly beaten egg whites into mixture. Cover bowl again and stand for 15 minutes.

Heat a small frying or crêpe pan over a medium heat. Spoon 2–3 tablespoonfuls of batter into pan at a time. Cook over medium heat until underside is lightly golden brown. Turn over and cook on other sides.

Serve warm with sour cream and smoked salmon or caviar, lumpfish roe, salmon roe or any smoked fish pâté and chopped hard-boiled egg white, raw onion, finely sliced spring onion, parsley and sieved hard-boiled egg yolk. It makes an interesting help-yourself first course or it could be extended with a salad.

**Serves 4–6**

# BASIC PIZZA

*1 teaspoon sugar*
*1 cup warm water*
*1 teaspoon active dry yeast granules*
*3 cups flour*
*1 teaspoon salt*
*¼ cup olive oil*

**SMOKED SALMON AND CAMEMBERT PIZZA WITH FRESH DILL.** *I also love topping a hot-from-the-oven pizza with fresh raw vegetables and herbs to garnish. It's like enjoying a salad and a pizza all in a mouthful.*

Whisk the sugar into the warm water and sprinkle the yeast granules over. Set aside for 10–15 minutes until the mixture is frothy.

In a large bowl, mix the flour and salt together. Make a well in the middle, then stir in the yeast mixture and olive oil. Mix with a wooden spoon to form a soft dough, then, using your hands, knead the dough for 5 minutes or so until it feels smooth and silky. This can also be done in the food processor. Flours vary in the amount of water they absorb so add a little extra if necessary, sprinkling over the surface of the dough until no stickiness remains. Remove the dough so that you can lightly oil the bowl then put the dough back in, covering the bowl with cling film.

Leave in a warm place, such as a windowsill in the sun or the hot water cupboard, to rise. The dough should puff up like a pillow to at least double its original size. Don't be concerned too much with the time to rise — it's the volume you measure, and a warm atmosphere produces this more quickly than a cold place. About 2–3 hours is usual.

Punch the dough down and knead for a further 2–3 minutes, then smooth it out, pushing it into a circular shape to fit a special pizza tin, a deep-dish pizza pan, or a lightly oiled baking tray.

Let the dough rise in the pan or on the tray for a further 20 minutes. Prick all over with a fork. Brush the dough with olive oil.

Now add the topping. Choose from one of those listed after this recipe or make up your own.

Bake in a preheated oven at 250°C for 10–15 minutes until the crust is crispy and golden-coloured and any cheese used has melted. Different toppings take different times in the oven and deep-dish-type pizzas take longest, about 30 minutes.

For a deep, crusty pizza with a moist topping, prebake the crust for approximately 5 minutes. Quickly add the topping and return to the hot oven.

### Suggested Toppings:

- Tasty cheese base topped with roast wild duck and orange
- Turkey or chicken on a tasty cheese base garnished with red-currant jelly or cranberry sauce
- Chicken with plum chutney and Brie cheese
- Avocado and fresh basil on a crispy cheese base
- Mild Cheddar cheese topped with crayfish and sprinkled with lemon juice and watercress
- Ham or bacon with cheese and crushed pineapple

## PIZZA

*Pizza is one of the world's favourite foods and New Zealanders love it as much as any native of Naples, from where the pizza is thought to originate. This recipe is for the new-style pizzas made so popular by chefs in California. I've worked out an easy base recipe and added ideas for toppings to show off our fabulous local foods.*

# SMOKED SALMON AND CAMEMBERT PIZZA WITH FRESH DILL

*500 g Camembert or a combination of grated
    Cheddar and sliced Camembert cheese
1 small red onion, peeled and finely sliced
200 g sliced smoked salmon
¼ cup olive oil
sour cream and fresh dill to garnish*

Bake the pizza crust for 6 minutes until just beginning to brown. Meanwhile derind and slice Camembert. Remove crust from oven and top with Camembert, leaving 0.5–1 cm border. Arrange onion and salmon on top and drizzle with half of the olive oil. Return to hot oven and bake until crust is golden brown and puffy and topping is heated through, approximately another 4–5 minutes.

Remove from oven to a cutting board, brush crust lightly with remaining olive oil and garnish with dollops of sour cream and fresh dill. A little caviar is a nice touch for a party pizza.

# GARLIC MUSSEL AND PIPI TOPPING

*4 cups grated Cheddar cheese, approximately
2 cups mixed fresh mussels and pipis
6–8 cloves garlic, crushed
2 tablespoons olive oil
salt and freshly ground black pepper
a little extra olive oil
grated Parmesan cheese, fresh parsley or
    coriander and crushed dried red chilli
    pepper to garnish*

Follow basic pizza directions then top dough with the grated cheese leaving a 1 cm border around the edge. Arrange mussels and pipis on top. Mix the crushed garlic and oil together and drizzle over surface evenly. Sprinkle with salt and pepper.

Bake according to the basic recipe instructions. After baking, remove from oven to a cutting board. Lightly brush the edge of the crust with olive oil, sprinkle the top with Parmesan cheese, herbs and chilli pepper to taste. Slice and serve immediately.

# WATER CHESTNUT, PICKLED ONION AND FRESH THYME PICNIC PIE

*This pie is best eaten the day you bake it although it does reheat well and can also be eaten cold.*

1 packet pre-rolled flaky pastry sheets
3 cups tasty cheese, grated
6 medium-sized pickled onions, finely sliced
2 teaspoons fresh thyme, or other fresh herbs,
    finely chopped
225 g can water chestnuts
salt and freshly ground black pepper to taste
8 large eggs
extra egg yolk for glazing
2 teaspoons water

Line a well-greased or non-stick pie dish or baking tin with the pre-rolled sheets of flaky pastry, carefully sealing any joins.

Sprinkle the pastry with 1 cup of the grated cheese and then layer the pickled onion, herbs, water chestnuts and cheese. Finish with a cheese layer and season with salt and pepper. Break the eggs, piercing the yolks, over the filling.

Cover the filling with a sheet of pastry and seal the edges carefully, using a little water to secure them tightly. Any pastry scraps can be used to decorate the top of the pie. Prick the top of the pie with a fork and brush generously with an egg wash made by mixing the extra egg yolk with 2 teaspoons water.

Bake at 200°C for 15 minutes then turn the oven down to 180°C and bake for a further hour until the pie is golden brown, well risen and firm and set in the middle. Bake a little longer if you are unsure. Cool in the pie tin then carefully remove to a board for cutting into portions.

**Serves 6–8**

# CHEESE ROULADE WITH SPICY CHICKEN AND PEANUT FILLING

75 g butter
⅓ cup flour
1½ cups milk
4 eggs, separated
1½ cups grated tasty Cheddar cheese
¼ teaspoon cream of tartar
salt and pepper to taste

Preheat oven to 220°C. Melt the butter in a saucepan, stir in flour and whisk in milk. Cook until smooth and thick. Stir in egg yolks, one at a time, then add grated cheese. Season with salt and pepper. Stir until smooth. In a separate bowl beat the egg whites and cream of tartar until stiff. Fold into the cheese mixture. Pour into a well-greased and paper-lined sponge roll tin, 23×35 cm. Bake for 15 minutes.

Remove the roulade from oven and gently turn out on to a wet, well wrung-out tea towel. Lift off the baking tin and peel the paper away. Trim off any rough edges and spread with the Spicy Chicken and Peanut Filling. Roll up the roulade like a sponge roll.

SPICY CHICKEN AND PEANUT FILLING

½ cup crunchy peanut butter
1 teaspoon chilli sauce (or to taste)
150 g sour cream
1 cup shredded or diced cooked chicken
   meat
2 tablespoons chopped parsley
freshly ground pepper to taste

In a small saucepan mix peanut butter, chilli sauce and sour cream. Stir until smooth. Fold in chicken meat and parsley and spread on to the roulade before rolling up.

**Serves 6**

# SPINACH ROULADE WITH BLUE CHEESE AND WALNUT FILLING

500 g fresh spinach
75 g butter
⅓ cup flour
1½ cups milk
4 eggs, separated
salt and pepper
¼ teaspoon cream of tartar

Wash spinach thoroughly and either microwave or steam over boiling water until wilted. Drain and squeeze dry, chop or whiz in a food processor.

Melt butter in a saucepan. Stir in flour and whisk in milk. Cook until smooth and thick. Stir in egg yolks one at a time, then add spinach, salt and pepper.

Beat egg whites and cream of tartar until stiff. Fold in the spinach mixture. Pour into a well-greased and paper-lined sponge roll tin, 23×35 cm. Bake in a preheated oven at 220°C for 15 minutes.

Remove the roulade from oven and turn out on to a wet, well wrung-out tea towel. Lift off baking tin and peel paper away. Trim any rough edges and spread with Spinach Roulade Filling. Use the tea towel to help you roll the roulade like a sponge roll.

SPINACH ROULADE FILLING

200 g firm blue cheese
250 g sour cream
½ cup chopped fresh walnuts
extra walnuts and fresh herbs to garnish

Crumble blue cheese and mix with sour cream, reserving a little for garnish. Spread over the cooled roulade and sprinkle with chopped walnuts. Roll up tightly then wrap in cling film. Keep refrigerated until ready to serve (can be prepared up to a day ahead). To serve, remove cling film and slice with a serrated knife, wiping the blade after each slice. Arrange on serving plates and microwave for 1–2 minutes on High to heat through. Spread remaining cheese mixture over top and garnish.

**Serves 6**

# SMOKED SALMON AND AVOCADO-LAYERED MOUSSE

### AVOCADO LAYER

2 ripe avocados
2 teaspoons gelatine
50 ml hot water
2 tablespoons fresh lemon juice
1 tablespoon finely chopped onion
2–3 drops hot pepper or Tabasco sauce
3 tablespoons finely chopped parsley
¼ teaspoon salt

### SALMON LAYER

300 g, approximately, smoked salmon offcuts
50 ml hot water
2 teaspoons gelatine
250 g sour cream
1 tablespoon tomato purée
½ cup good quality mayonnaise
2–3 drops hot pepper sauce or Tabasco sauce
1 tablespoon finely chopped onion
½ cup finely chopped celery
¼ teaspoon salt
wedges of lemon and sprigs of fresh herbs to
    garnish (optional)

*Canned salmon or any variety of boneless smoked fish can be substituted for the salmon.*

Line a loaf tin or glass loaf mould with cling film. To make avocado layer, purée avocado flesh in a food processor or blender. Dissolve gelatine in the hot water and add to avocado in food processor. Add other ingredients and mix together until well blended and smooth. Spoon into the lined loaf tin or glass loaf mould. Wash food processor bowl for next step.

To make salmon layer, purée salmon in the food processor. Dissolve gelatine in the hot water and add to salmon in food processor. Add other ingredients and process until well blended and smooth. Spoon over avocado layer, smoothing the surface. Gently tap the tin or mould to remove air bubbles and settle the mixture. Refrigerate for several hours or overnight until firmly set.

Gently turn out and cut into thick slices. Serve on a small bed of salad greens and leaves, garnish with wedges of lemon and sprigs of fresh herbs, if desired.

### Serves 6

*You can make different fillings for **SPINACH ROULADE** (page 37) according to your own taste. The roulade pictured is filled with a simple blend of smoked trout, sour cream and freshly ground black pepper.*

*A salad with chunks of blue cheese, toasted pecan nuts, cherry tomatoes and crispy croutons tossed with* **CLASSIC VINAIGRETTE DRESSING** *(page 53) makes a great start to a meal.*

# ZUCCHINI, CARROT AND PEANUT LOAF

2 tablespoons oil
1 large onion, finely chopped
½ cup unsalted peanuts, roughly chopped
1 cup scrubbed and grated zucchini
1 cup scrubbed and grated carrot
½ cup rolled oats
2 tablespoons coconut
1 tablespoon tomato purée
3 eggs, lightly beaten
½ cup fresh breadcrumbs
2 tablespoons chopped parsley or a
    combination of fresh herbs
½ teaspoon salt and freshly ground black
    pepper

Heat oil in a large frypan. Add onion and cook for a few minutes until soft. Stir in the peanuts, zucchini and carrot. Cook, stirring for about 5 minutes. Add the remaining ingredients, mixing well. Spoon into a 12×22 cm well-greased and tinfoil- or paper-lined loaf tin.

Bake at 180°C for 35–40 minutes until loaf is firm and set in the middle and the top is nicely golden brown.

Cool in the tin for 5 minutes then turn out on to a serving plate. Serve with peanut sauce and a crisp green salad.

## EASY PEANUT SAUCE

An easy peanut sauce can be made by mixing 4 tablespoons crunchy peanut butter with 150 g sour cream. Gently warm this combination in a small pan, or microwave it, whisking until smooth. Add approximately 1 teaspoon sweet chilli sauce to taste. Add salt and pepper and thin to desired consistency with a little milk or cream. Spoon over loaf slices and garnish with chopped nuts and a sprig of fresh herbs.

***Serves 6–8***

## GREEN-BASED SALAD

A salad for a first course is a great way to start a meal. I particularly like serving hot items like crispy bacon or panfried chicken livers over a crisp, cold salad base. The key to success is simplicity and really good flavours. When you have only a small portion of a luxury ingredient, for example scallops, a salad is a great way to extend the scallops so that everyone gets a taste.

Here are some favourite salad combinations of mine.

Over a green salad leaf base using any of different lettuce varieties, young small spinach leaves, celery leaves, watercress, herbs, chicory, and sprouts, try:

- Chunks of blue cheese, toasted pecan nuts and crispy croutons with Classic Vinaigrette Dressing
- Crispy oven-cooked bacon and roasted water chestnuts garnished with tiny red cherry tomatoes and a basil dressing
- Scallops panfried lightly in butter with grated fresh ginger and an orange and ginger dressing
- Diced avocado, hot baby potatoes and crispy bacon and a sour cream dressing
- Cubed steamed kumara and orange segments with an Oriental sesame dressing and sesame seeds
- Slices of cold cooked potatoes, red onion rings and salami or cold sliced sausage with a blue cheese dressing
- Blanched green beans, strawberries and sliced button mushrooms with a strawberry-flavoured vinaigrette and pine nuts.

## FAVOURITE POTATO SALADS

*The best sort of potatoes for potato salads are new, waxy potatoes. They don't crumble but keep their shape and will not absorb an excessive amount of dressing which can make a potato salad squishy. Dressing the salad when it's warm or at room temperature, not chilled, helps with developing the flavours of the dressing. Pouring the dressing over and gently tossing or mixing helps avoid the sticky, gluey mush so often served up in cafeteria 'salad' bars.*

# CURRIED POTATO SALAD WITH TOASTED CUMIN

500 g small potatoes, scrubbed or peeled
3 spring onions, sliced
1 cup natural yoghurt
1 teaspoon curry powder
1 teaspoon sweet chilli sauce
1 teaspoon toasted cumin seeds to garnish

Cut the potatoes into cubes, cover with cold salted water and bring to the boil. Simmer for 5 minutes until just soft. Drain and cool to room temperature.

Place cold potatoes in a serving dish and sprinkle with spring onions. Mix yoghurt, curry powder and sweet chilli sauce together and pour over the potatoes. Mix gently and garnish with cumin seeds.

# DILLED RED POTATO SALAD

500 g small red potatoes, scrubbed
½ teaspoon French-style mustard
1 tablespoon white wine vinegar
2 teaspoons white wine
salt and freshly ground black pepper to taste
2 tablespoons oil
¼ cup finely chopped fresh dill

Cut the potatoes in quarters and steam for 7–10 minutes until just tender. In a bowl whisk together the mustard, vinegar, wine, salt and pepper. Add the oil, whisking until it's well mixed.

Toss the warm potatoes in this dressing until they're well coated, and sprinkle with the dill. Add more pepper to taste. Let the potato salad stand for at least 30 minutes for the flavours to develop.

# BLUE CHEESE AND BACON POTATO SALAD

500 g tiny new waxy potatoes, scrubbed
5–6 rashers of bacon
250 g sour cream
¼ cup white wine vinegar
200 g crumbly blue cheese such as Ferndale
   Blue Supreme
salt and freshly ground black pepper to taste
2 spring onions, chopped, including green tips
3 tablespoons chopped chives, including a few
   of the flowers if available

Steam the baby potatoes until just tender, about 7–10 minutes. Meanwhile oven-bake bacon until crisp and crumble when cool.

Process or blend the sour cream and white wine vinegar, add half the blue cheese and mix until smooth. Season with salt and pepper to taste.

Toss the potatoes, onions and chives in this dressing and garnish with bacon and remaining crumbled blue cheese. Rest the salad for at least 30 minutes before eating to allow the blue cheese flavour to permeate through the potatoes.

Concord
Potatoes
$2.50 bag

Carrots.
$1.00 bag

Quality

FAR NORTH

Red oak &

# VEGETABLES AND
# SIDE DISHES

*I frequently plan a meal around my supply of fresh seasonal vegetables. Good cooks are often keen gardeners (even urban dwellers in high-rise apartments can cultivate their own herbs, lettuces etc. on windowsills and balconies), with a well-developed sense of what's in season and the knowledge of how to utilise produce to the fullest.*

*Even if you don't grow your own vegetables, take time out now and then to pod fresh peas, husk corn etc. — it's good for the soul. My love for fresh vegetables goes back to the days when my father was a grower in Hawke's Bay back in the 1950s and 60s and one of the first to grow zucchini and capsicums commercially in this country. We had a never-ending supply of these and other fresh vegetables which my mother would cook in lots of different ways. She had a herb garden long before it was fashionable and the addition of fresh herbs made for some interesting experiments.*

*These days growers are constantly striving for the elusive all-purpose, all-season, disease-resistant, heavy-cropping, long-keeping super vegetable but often, when all these criteria are met, the flavour is lost in the process. Customer pressure can change marketing practices and you can contribute by pestering your greengrocer or vegetable supplier into having varieties and qualities identified at the point of sale as a matter of course. This applies particularly to potatoes. I follow the rule that if it's grown underground (carrots, potatoes, etc.) in the "cold and dark" the vegetable should be cooked "cold and dark" — i.e. in cold water brought up to the boil with the lid on.*

*Many of the dishes in this chapter can make a meal in themselves if you just add a salad, bread, cheese and fruit.*

## KUMARA AND CASHEW FRITTERS

*1 egg, lightly beaten*
*1 cup self-raising flour*
*½ teaspoon salt*
*freshly ground black pepper to taste*
*1 cup diced, steamed kumara*
*3 tablespoons chopped toasted cashews*
*milk for mixing*
*oil for frying*
*chopped parsley or fresh herbs (optional)*

Combine ingredients in a bowl and add just enough milk to combine — don't overmix. Heat oil, about 1 cm deep, in a heavy frypan, preferably non-stick, until hot. Drop small spoonfuls of batter into oil. Turn when underside of fritter is golden brown and cook on other side. Drain on paper towels and serve warm.

**Makes about 6–8**

## CHILLI SWEETCORN FRITTERS

*1 egg, lightly beaten*
*1 cup self-raising flour*
*½ teaspoon salt*
*freshly ground black pepper to taste*
*1 cup cream-style whole kernel or fresh or*
  *frozen corn kernels*
*1 teaspoon sweet chilli sauce*
*milk for mixing*
*oil for frying*
*chopped parsley or fresh herbs (optional)*

Combine ingredients in a bowl and add just enough milk to combine — don't overmix. Heat oil, about 1 cm deep, in a heavy frypan, preferably non-stick, until hot. Drop small spoonfuls of batter into oil. Turn when underside of fritter is golden brown and cook on other side. Drain on paper towels and serve warm.

**Makes about 6–8**

## CARROT AND PARSNIP FRITTERS

*1 egg, lightly beaten*
*1 cup self-raising flour*
*½ teaspoon salt*
*freshly ground black pepper to taste*
*1 cup steamed carrot and parsnip, mashed*
*milk for mixing*
*oil for frying*
*chopped parsley or fresh herbs (optional)*

Combine ingredients in a bowl and add just enough milk to combine — don't overmix. Heat oil, about 1 cm deep, in a heavy frypan, preferably non-stick, until hot. Drop small spoonfuls of batter into oil. Turn when underside of fritter is golden brown and cook on other side. Drain on paper towels and serve warm.

**Makes about 6–8**

## CRISPY FRIED VEGETABLE SKINS

Serve as a nibble with drinks or as a snack meal with a sauce, sour cream or a fresh fruity chilli salsa. They are also a really good accompaniment to game and hot lamb dishes. You can use all kinds of root vegetables, including potatoes, red and golden kumaras, parsnips, Jerusalem artichokes, swedes and turnips, and carrots of different varieties.

Kumaras and parsnips take hardly any time to crisp and cook golden brown and potatoes take the longest. Potato skins crisp up best if they're dry-roasted for approximately 15 minutes in a hot oven until just soft. All other vegetables are best deep-fried from raw.

Heat oil or fat as hot as you'd have it for potato chips and deep-fry skins in small batches. Drain on a tray and reheat by plunging back into the hot oil for a few seconds. Drain on paper towels and season with salt and freshly ground black pepper to taste.

## CRISPY GARLIC POTATOES

*1 medium-sized potato per person*
*oil for coating*
*garlic salt*
*chopped parsley*

Scrub potatoes, do not peel, and chop roughly into 2 cm cubes. Place cubed potatoes in a roasting dish, sprinkle with oil so that they are lightly coated, then dust with garlic salt. Roast in a medium-hot oven, 180–190°C, for 25–30 minutes until crispy and golden. Toss in chopped parsley before serving.

## BAKED ONION HALVES

This is a really easy way to bake onions, taking only 2 minutes to prepare, but they always get heaps of compliments.

Cut required number of onions in half through the top to the roots. Don't peel off any of the outer papery skins. Place cut-side down on a lightly oiled baking tray and bake for 30–40 minutes until cooked through and golden on the cut surface.

Serve with roasts or grilled meats and game etc. The sweet and mild-tasting onion flesh should be eaten out of the skin.

# SWEETCORN AND ZUCCHINI LOAF

*A loaf or slice is a really interesting way to serve vegetables. Green capsicum, grated parsnip or carrot, etc., can be substituted for the sweetcorn and zucchini.*

*1 kg zucchini, grated*
*1 tablespoon salt*
*50 g butter*
*4 spring onions, finely chopped*
*salt and freshly ground black pepper*
*4 eggs*
*300 ml cream*
*300 g corn kernels (fresh, frozen or canned)*

Place zucchini in a mixing bowl and sprinkle with the salt, tossing to mix well. Cover and set aside for an hour to remove excess liquid. Rinse zucchini and wring out in paper towels or a clean tea towel to remove all excess water.

Melt butter in a large heavy frypan, add spring onion and zucchini and cook over a medium heat for approximately 10 minutes, until zucchini is soft. Season to taste with salt and pepper.

Beat eggs and cream together, and stir in corn kernels. Add spring onion and zucchini and mix well.

Pour mixture into a greased and paper-lined 7-cup loaf tin. Place tin in a baking dish and pour in enough water to come three-quarters of the way up the sides of the loaf tin.

Bake at 180°C for 1¼ hours until firm and set. Cool for 10 minutes in the tin, then carefully tip out on to a serving plate. Serve as a light vegetable dish on its own, or as a vegetable accompaniment to a main course.

**Serves 6–8**

*We grow masses of zucchini at home and this*
**SWEETCORN AND ZUCCHINI LOAF** *is a good way to use them when we have an excess supply in summer. Treat it as a master recipe and experiment with other vegetables to gain different flavours and textures.*

Above: *The New Zealand countryside is dotted with stalls like this and my family love going on weekend drives to stock up on fresh produce.*

Right: **WILD RICE PANCAKES** *served with glossy fresh asparagus can make a tasty meal on its own.*

# WILD RICE PANCAKES

*2 eggs, separated*
*1 cup milk*
*50 g butter, melted*
*1 cup self-raising flour*
*½ teaspoon salt*
*100 g wild rice, cooked*
*1 tablespoon finely chopped parsley*
*a little oil for frying*

Beat egg yolks and milk together in a large bowl. Add melted butter then stir in flour and salt and mix to a smooth batter. Stir in rice and parsley and then fold in stiffly whipped egg whites.

Heat oil in a non-stick crêpe pan, pour in a small ladle of mixture and cook the pancake until golden on the underside. Turn over and cook on other side. Keep cooked pancakes covered and warm while you cook remaining batter.

*Makes 6–8*

## POTATO AU GRATIN

6–8 large potatoes
2 cups grated cheese
salt and freshly ground black pepper
1 teaspoon dried thyme (optional)
3–4 cloves garlic, crushed (optional)
200 ml cream

Scrub potatoes and boil until just cooked but still firm. Drain and allow to cool slightly before slicing thinly. In an ovenproof dish, layer sliced potato with grated cheese (leaving some for the top), salt and pepper, thyme and garlic. Pour cream over so that it comes approximately one-quarter of the way up the dish. Sprinkle top generously with grated cheese and bake at 180°C for 30–40 minutes until golden brown.

**Serves 6 generous portions**

## MUSTARD BATTER ONION RINGS

2 large onions, cut into 5 mm slices
½ cup flour
1 teaspoon salt
½ teaspoon freshly ground black pepper
2 tablespoons French-style mustard
½ cup soda water or sparkling mineral water

Separate the onion slices into rings and soak in cold water and ice for 10–15 minutes.

Whisk together flour, salt and pepper, mustard and soda water. Mix until smooth and well blended.

Drain onion rings and pat dry on paper towels. Dip them into the batter coating and let excess drip off.

Deep fry in batches in oil at 190°C. Turn over and cook for about 3 minutes until puffed, golden, and crispy. Drain on paper towels and keep warm, uncovered in the oven, until all the rings are cooked.

**Makes about 12–15**

## BROAD BEANS WITH BACON, CREAM AND SAGE

3–4 slices lean bacon
500 g broad beans, fresh or thawed frozen
150 ml cream
salt and freshly ground black pepper
1 teaspoon chopped fresh sage leaves or
    ¼ teaspoon dried
2 tablespoons chopped parsley

In a large frypan, cook bacon until crisp, add beans and cover with cream. Add lots of pepper and salt to taste and sprinkle over sage leaves. Cook for approximately 10 minutes over a medium heat, until the beans are softened and the cream reduced. Stir through parsley before serving.

**Serves 4–6**

# ASPARAGUS WITH LEMON HOLLANDAISE

Peel the cut ends of the asparagus spears. I know this sounds fiddly, but it makes all the difference and saves wastage as most of the woody stems can be eaten when the hard, outer fibre is peeled away. You can become quite quick at the job and obviously any pencil-thin spears don't need to be peeled. Cook asparagus in boiling salted water until just tender. Loosely tying the spears and standing them cut-side down in the water to cook is a good idea.

Drain asparagus and pour the Lemon Hollandaise over. Garnish with shaved fresh Parmesan cheese, chopped herbs or toasted sesame seeds.

## LEMON HOLLANDAISE

3 egg yolks
grated zest of 1 large lemon
¼ cup fresh lemon juice
250 g butter
salt and freshly ground black pepper

Whiz egg yolks, lemon zest and juice in a food blender or food processor. With motor running, pour in the just-melted butter in a steady stream. Add salt and pepper to taste. Serve immediately, or keep warm over a bowl of hot water.

**Makes 1 cup**

# RED CABBAGE, APPLES AND RAISINS

½ red cabbage
50 g butter
2 apples, peeled and sliced
½ teaspoon caraway seeds
50 g seedless raisins
50 g currants
2 teaspoons sugar
3 tablespoons malt vinegar
1 tablespoon mustard seeds
salt and freshly ground black pepper
grated zest and juice of 1 large lemon

Finely shred cabbage, removing core and thick ribs. Melt butter in a large saucepan. Add apple, caraway seeds, raisins and currants. Cook, stirring, for a couple of minutes. Add cabbage, tossing and stirring, and cook for 5 minutes. Add sugar and vinegar. With lid on saucepan, cook for 30 minutes over a gentle heat. Add mustard seeds, salt and pepper, lemon juice and zest. Toss together and serve.

**Serves 4–6**

# STUFFED FIELD MUSHROOMS

*These are great as a side dish to accompany a rich, meaty main course. They also make a good vegetarian side dish or first course.*

*Use large, flat field mushrooms which have a good earthy flavour. They're easier to stuff and keep their shape well when cooked. However, larger opened button mushrooms are a good alternative if you can't get fresh field ones.*

6 large field mushrooms
50 g butter
1 large onion, finely chopped
4 cloves garlic, crushed
¼ cup pine nuts
1 cup fresh brown breadcrumbs
1 tablespoon fresh chopped herbs
salt and freshly ground black pepper

Wipe mushrooms clean and remove and discard stalks. Lay mushrooms in an oven dish. Melt butter in a frypan and sauté the onion and garlic until soft but not brown. Add the pine nuts, then breadcrumbs and herbs. Season with salt and pepper.

Fill mushroom caps with this mixture and bake at 180°C for about 20 minutes until heated through. Serve hot.

**Serves 6**

**STUFFED FIELD MUSHROOMS** *remind me of my childhood on the farm. Our friends from town would come out in droves to pick them and we always finished up with a hearty afternoon tea to reward everyone's efforts.*

## WILD RICE SALAD

2 cups long grain white rice, cooked and rinsed
½ cup wild rice, cooked and rinsed
2 cups brown rice, cooked and rinsed
1 red capsicum, seeded and finely diced
1 green capsicum, seeded and finely diced
3 spring onions, finely chopped, including the
    green leaves
½ cup chopped parsley and chives
½ cup toasted sunflower seeds

DRESSING

1 cup soya oil
⅓ cup white wine vinegar
1 tablespoon whole-grain mustard
½ teaspoon salt
freshly ground black pepper to taste
½ teaspoon sweet chilli sauce
grated zest and juice of 1 lemon

Mix together all the rices, capsicums, spring onion, herbs and sunflower seeds, then add the dressing and toss well.

Mix all dressing ingredients in a blender or food processor.

**Serves 6–8**

## SPINACH TORTELLINI AND CHERRY TOMATO SALAD

500 g spinach tortellini, cooked, rinsed and
    tossed in 1 tablespoon light salad oil
2 spring onions, finely chopped
3 tablespoons finely chopped fresh herbs
2 cups cherry tomatoes
extra chopped herbs to garnish

DRESSING

½ cup oil
3 tablespoons white wine vinegar
1 teaspoon prepared whole-grain mustard
salt and freshly ground black pepper to taste

Mix all dressing ingredients in a blender or food processor. Toss salad ingredients together in the dressing and then garnish with extra chopped fresh herbs.

**Serves 6–8**

## CUCUMBER, YOGHURT AND MINT SALAD

*This is a great side dish for hot spicy foods or a good sauce for fish, or chicken, especially barbecued salmon steaks or plain grilled chicken breasts when you need something with a bit of zing to liven them up. Try it as a tasty dip for pita bread, nacho chips, etc. as well.*

1 telegraph cucumber
salt and freshly ground black pepper
2 cloves garlic, peeled and crushed
450 g thick natural unsweetened yoghurt
2 tablespoons olive oil
1 teaspoon white wine vinegar
1 tablespoon finely chopped fresh mint

Peel the cucumber, cut in half lengthways and scoop out seeds with a teaspoon. Finely dice the two lengths, place in a single layer on a plate or shallow dish and sprinkle generously with salt. Allow to stand for approximately an hour, then rinse cucumber pieces in cold water and dry on paper towels. This removes any bitter juice.

Mix remaining ingredients together and check the seasoning, adding salt and pepper to taste. Refrigerate for a further hour or so for the flavours to blend and develop.

**Serves 4–6**

## BULGUR WHEAT SALAD

*This is a handy salad to have in your repertoire when there are no fresh salad leaves available. It works well on a boat trip when the lettuce has run out. It'll keep scurvy at bay as it's bursting with colour and flavour and the sharp lemon taste is very refreshing.*

1 cup bulgur wheat
6 medium-sized ripe outdoor tomatoes
6 spring onions
1 small telegraph cucumber
½ cup chopped parsley
1 tablespoon finely chopped mint
grated zest and juice of 2 medium-sized
　　lemons
3 tablespoons olive oil
salt and freshly ground black pepper

Soak wheat in cold water for an hour. Drain in a sieve and press down to squeeze out excess water. Spread wheat out on paper towels or a clean tea towel to dry while you prepare the rest of the ingredients.

Scald tomatoes in boiling water and peel away the skins. Halve and remove seeds, then chop up tomato flesh into fine dice. Finely chop spring onions, both the green and white parts. Cut cucumber in half lengthways but do not peel. Scoop out seeds with a teaspoon then finely dice the two lengths. Mix remaining ingredients together, tossing well to coat with the oil and lemon juice. Season to taste with salt and pepper. Cover and chill for at least an hour.

**Serves 4–6**

# MAYONNAISE

*2 large egg yolks, at room temperature*
*2 teaspoons white wine vinegar*
*1 teaspoon French-style mustard, or to taste*
*¼ teaspoon salt*
*white pepper to taste*
*1½ cups olive oil, vegetable oil, or a*
*    combination*
*fresh lemon juice to taste*
*cream to thin the mayonnaise, if desired*

In a blender or food processor combine the egg yolks, 1 teaspoon of the vinegar, mustard, salt, and white pepper. Process until well combined and add ½ cup of the oil, drop by drop, beating constantly. Add the remaining teaspoon of vinegar and the remaining cup of oil in a stream, beating constantly. Add the lemon juice and white pepper and salt to taste, and thin the mayonnaise with the cream or water.

**Makes 2 cups**

# CLASSIC VINAIGRETTE DRESSING

*The golden rule with vinaigrette dressings is to be generous with the oil and miserly with the vinegar. I prefer 50/50 extra virgin olive oil and soya oil.*

*¼ cup white wine vinegar*
*2 teaspoons French or smooth-style mustard*
*¾ cup oil*
*salt and freshly ground black pepper to taste*

Whisk all ingredients until well mixed. I make vinaigrette in a blender to get a really good emulsified brew.

**Variations:**

There are countless variations on this basic recipe. The vinegar can be red or white wine vinegar, sherry vinegar, a herb-flavoured vinegar, such as tarragon, or a fruit vinegar, such as raspberry or peach, either used alone or with a dash of balsamic vinegar. You could replace the vinegar entirely with lemon, orange or lime juice. The mustard could be whole-grain type, or hot English. Instead of olive oil, you could use walnut, hazelnut or avocado oil. For a milder-tasting vinaigrette try soya, sunflower or grapeseed oil. Make your own distinctive-flavoured dressings by including the following combinations:
• Olive and coriander
• Orange and ginger
• Anchovy
• Blue cheese — crumbled blue cheese and a little cream
• Oriental — sesame oil and toasted sesame seeds
• Sour cream — add 150 ml sour cream to the mixture.

**Makes about 1 cup**

## CITRUS BEANS

*500 g green beans, trimmed*
*juice and zest of 2 oranges*
*100 g butter*
*1 teaspoon chopped parsley*
*salt and freshly ground black pepper*

Cook the beans in boiling water until crisp-tender, about 2 minutes. Refresh under cold running water. Heat the orange juice and zest and the butter in a large frypan or saucepan. Add the beans and toss until warmed through. Sprinkle with chopped parsley and season to taste.

**Serves 4**

## LEMON CHIVE FETTUCINE WITH CAPSICUMS

*500 g fettucine noodles, fresh or frozen*
*100 g butter*
*¼ cup extra virgin olive oil*
*4–5 cloves garlic, peeled and crushed*
*1 cup sliced red, green and yellow capsicums*
*½ cup chopped fresh chives*
*a handful of parsley, chopped*
*juice and zest of 2 lemons*
*1 teaspoon lemon pepper seasoning*

Cook the fettucine until tender in a large pot with plenty of boiling salted water. While the fettucine is cooking, heat the butter and oil together in a large frypan. Add the garlic and cook for 30–40 seconds to soften. Add capsicums, parsley, lemon juice and zest and seasoning. Stir and cook over a medium heat for 2–3 minutes to warm through. Drain fettucine and toss with capsicum sauce. Serve immediately.

**Serves 4**

**LEMON CHIVE FETTUCINE WITH CAPSICUMS** *makes an exciting change to a plain pasta or potato accompaniment to a meal. The colours are really vibrant and the lemon juice and zest add a surprise but welcome flavour to this dish.*

*New Zealand onions have gained a worldwide reputation for their superb quality and this tart is a great way to serve them when you want to dress them up a bit.*

# ONION TART

*Crispy pastry with a peppery cream onion filling — this tart makes a hearty vegetable side dish or an excellent meal on its own.*

2 cups flour
½ teaspoon salt
200 g butter
1 egg yolk
3–4 tablespoons ice-cold water

In a food processor mix the flour, salt and butter until the mixture resembles coarse breadcrumbs. Tip out into a large bowl. Mix the egg yolk and water together and sprinkle over crumb mixture in the bowl. Stirring to combine, knead lightly with your fingers until the pastry clings together in a smooth ball. Wrap in plastic film and chill for 30 minutes.

Roll out on a floured board and press into a 20–23 cm pie dish or flan ring. Chill again.

ONION FILLING

100 g butter
1 tablespoon oil
6–8 medium-sized onions, peeled and
  coarsely chopped
4 egg yolks
150 ml cream
salt and fresh ground black pepper

Melt the butter in a large saucepan and add the oil and chopped onions. Stir over a medium heat and allow onion to cook until softened and just lightly coloured, about 20 minutes, then remove from heat. Beat egg yolks and cream together. Add salt and black pepper to taste and stir into the cooked onions. Pour mixture into the chilled pastry case and bake in a moderate oven, 180°C, until the filling is set and the pastry is golden and crisp. Serve warm.

**Serves 4–6**

# B R U S S E L S   S P R O U T S   W I T H   S O U R   C R E A M   A N D   G I N G E R E D   A L M O N D   C R U M B S

20–24 Brussels sprouts, trimmed
100 g butter
1 cup coarse fresh breadcrumbs
salt and freshly ground black pepper
½ teaspoon ground ginger
½ cup chopped blanched almonds
250 g sour cream

Cut an x into the stem of each sprout. Cook in boiling salted water until tender, about 10–15 minutes. Drain well. Chop each sprout in half. Transfer halved sprouts to a serving dish.

Melt the butter in a frypan over a medium heat. Add the breadcrumbs, seasoning, ground ginger and chopped almonds. Stir until all the butter is absorbed into the breadcrumbs and they are golden brown. Spoon the sour cream over the halved sprouts in the serving dish and then sprinkle with the crumb mixture. Serve immediately.

**Serves 4–6**

# K U M A R A   W I T H   O R A N G E   B U T T E R   A N D   F R E S H   T H Y M E

4–6 medium-sized kumara or sweet potatoes, peeled and cut into 1 cm slices
100 g butter
juice and zest of 1 orange
1 tablespoon chopped fresh thyme leaves
salt and pepper

Cook the sliced kumara in boiling salted water until tender, about 6–8 minutes. Drain well. Melt the butter in a large frypan or saucepan. Add the orange juice, zest and thyme. Toss the kumara in the orange butter, turning each slice so that it becomes well coated, and cook for 4–5 minutes. Season to taste and serve immediately.

**Serves 4**

# R O A S T E D   G A R L I C   P U R É E

This is a wonderful side dish to serve with roasted or grilled meat. The taste of the purée is quite mellow compared to garlic in its raw state. Simply place whole bulbs of fleshy garlic in an oiled baking dish and roast at 180–200°C for 35–40 minutes or until they are quite soft. When they are ready, remove from the dish and slice through the head of each bulb, taking the tops off each individual clove in the process. Squeeze out the garlic purée and discard the skins. Serve warm.

## BAKED STUFFED AUBERGINES

2 medium-sized aubergines
½ cup olive oil
2 cloves garlic, peeled and crushed
1 medium-sized onion, peeled and finely
    chopped
2 teaspoons chopped fresh oregano or
    ½ teaspoon dried
¼ cup chopped parsley
pinch chilli powder or a few drops Tabasco
    sauce
½ cup cooked rice
1 cup grated tasty cheese
2 tablespoons pine nuts
salt and pepper
50 g butter
½ cup fresh breadcrumbs
Parmesan cheese, grated

Cut the aubergines in half, lengthways. Using a spoon, scoop out the flesh leaving a shell about 4–5 mm thick. Roughly chop the aubergine flesh.

Heat the oil in a large frypan. Add the garlic and onion and fry over a medium heat for 1–2 minutes until softened. Stir in the chopped aubergine flesh and cook for 4–5 minutes, stirring constantly, until tender. Add the oregano, parsley, chilli, rice, tasty cheese and pine nuts. Toss to mix well, then season to taste. Fill each aubergine shell with this mixture.

Melt the butter in a small frypan. Stir in the breadcrumbs and cook for 2–3 minutes. Spoon the fried crumbs over each filled aubergine shell and sprinkle with Parmesan cheese. Place stuffed shells in a shallow baking dish with 1 cm of water in the bottom. Bake at 180°C for 40–45 minutes. Serve hot.

**Serves 4**

## PANFRIED CUCUMBER WITH SWEET CHILLI AND MINT

*A hint of chilli balances with cool mint giving a good flavour as well as an attractive colour to this dish.*

1 large telegraph cucumber
100 g butter
1 tablespoon olive oil
1 teaspoon sweet chilli sauce
salt and freshly ground black pepper
¼ cup finely chopped fresh mint

Peel the cucumber and cut in half, lengthways. Using a teaspoon, scoop out seeds and discard. Cut each of the two lengths into 1 cm slices.

Melt the butter in a large frypan. Add the oil and chilli sauce. Sauté the cucumber until softened and heated through, about 2–3 minutes. Season to taste and sprinkle with the chopped mint. Serve immediately.

**Serves 4**

# MEAT
# AND GAME

*When you're mad for meat and potatoes, then no amount of smoked salmon or pasta will offset the craving. It's got to be a good, thick steak or a roast dinner when the rumbling hunger sets in.*

*New Zealanders are a carnivorous bunch — early New Zealand settlers brought sheep, cattle and pigs to this country to satisfy their largely European tradition of eating meat at most meals. We still eat a lot of lamb and, as one of the largest exporters of sheep meat in the world, it's little wonder that we have developed some delicious lamb recipes to alleviate any monotony.*

*Some of these recipes were initially influenced by our European fore-bears but these days, it's more common to find Asian or Middle Eastern influences in our meat cuisine. This is evident in the use of spices, chilli, yoghurt and fresh herbs that I now use as a matter of course whether I'm cooking a traditional meat dish in the kitchen or preparing a barbecue outdoors.*

*I think we're really spoilt given the variety, quality and flavour of New Zealand meat compared to many other countries. Sometimes, when I've been visiting other parts of the world, I've been served paper-thin flavourless slices of unidentifiable meat, often with the texture of cardboard. It always makes me long for the thick, juicy cuts that I tend to take for granted back home.*

## MUTTON AND LAMB

*When I was visiting friends way up the Rakaia River Gorge in the high country of the South Island, we experienced some really fabulous roast mutton meals. The meat was cooked very much in the usual fashion, but more often than not it was quite well done — no pinkness remaining and the meat just falling away from the bone. The huge joint of roasted meat was removed from the oven and placed on a bed of rosemary and lavender branches to serve. The smell was just divine, the hot meat absorbing the scent of the greenery.*

*When meat was cooked on a barbecue outside, various different green woods were burnt on the coals to produce wonderful aromatic smoke which subtly flavoured the meat. Pine needles and small cones, eucalyptus or fruit tree and vine prunings, all give a lovely woody aroma and produce different intriguing flavours and, of course, the presentation was just sensational. The crispy nut-brown meat was surrounded by a garnish of whatever was used in its cooking or smoking, for example fresh pine needles and a sprinkling of pine nuts.*

*Lamb is cheap meat in New Zealand and many of us enjoy constantly inventing and modifying lamb recipes to alleviate the monotony. There are as many different ways of cooking lamb as there are culinary traditions. Its tender, richly flavoured meat can be complemented by a variety of herbs and spices and lamb, as well as mutton, lends itself to comforting hearty roast meals. The Mediterranean style of cooking lamb with olive oil, wine and tomatoes is as popular now as Oriental and Indian methods of slow simmering with perfumed and aromatic spices, fruits and yoghurt.*

*Generally lamb is best when still pink or medium rare but long slow cooking where the meat falls from the bones has its own special appeal as well.*

---

### MEAT COOKING TIMES AND TEMPERATURES

**Beef** — 15 minutes per 500 g in a hot oven (200°C) for rare; 20 minutes per 500 g for well-cooked.

**Lamb** — 20 minutes per 500 g in a hottish oven (190°C) for a pink centre; 25 minutes per 500 g for well-cooked.

**Veal** — 25 minutes per 500 g in a hottish oven (190°C).

**Pork** — 35 minutes per 500 g in a moderate oven (180°C).

**Turkey and Chicken** — 20 minutes per 500 g in a moderate oven (180°C).

# ROAST LEG OF LAMB WITH MUSTARD HERB CRUST

*2–3 kg leg of lamb*

## MUSTARD HERB CRUST

*4 tablespoons oil*
*4 tablespoons whole-grain or French-style*
  *mustard*
*2 tablespoons chopped parsley*
*1 small onion, finely chopped*
*1 tablespoon chopped fresh rosemary, or*
  *1 teaspoon dried*
*1 teaspoon chopped fresh marjoram or*
  *½ teaspoon dried*
*1 teaspoon chopped fresh oregano or*
  *½ teaspoon dried*
*1 teaspoon chopped fresh thyme or*
  *½ teaspoon dried*
*3 tablespoons dry white wine*
*1 cup fresh brown breadcrumbs*

Roast the lamb in a medium, 180°C, oven for approximately 20 minutes per 500 g or until cooked to your liking. About 10 minutes before it finishes cooking, mix together all the ingredients except for the breadcrumbs. Remove meat from the oven and spread the upper side with a thick layer of the mustard and herb mixture. Sprinkle over the breadcrumbs and return to the oven for the last 10 minutes of cooking and to allow the crust to crisp.

**Serves 4–6**

# GARLIC AND CUMIN-SCENTED LEG OF LAMB

*2–3 kg leg of lamb, trimmed and butterflied*
  *open*
*150 ml unsweetened natural yoghurt*
*1 medium-sized onion, finely chopped*
*juice and zest of 1 large lemon*
*3–4 cloves garlic, crushed*
*1 tablespoon grated fresh ginger*
*1 tablespoon ground cumin or crushed whole*
  *cumin seeds*
*1 tablespoon freshly ground black pepper*
*salt*

Prick the butterflied leg with a fork. Mix the rest of the ingredients together and spread over lamb. Cover and refrigerate for at least 4 hours, preferably overnight. Bring to room temperature before cooking.

Barbecue, grill or roast for approximately 20 minutes per 500 g or until meat is cooked to your liking. This lamb is delicious served with Greek-style Cucumber, Yoghurt and Mint Salad.

**Serves 4–6**

Right: **MARINATED LAMB LOINS** *are enhanced by a*
**PORT AND BLACKBERRY SAUCE.**

Opposite: *This Greek-influenced* **LAMB AND FETA CHEESE**
**SALAD** *is one of my favourite picnic meals. It's easy to
transport and you only need a fork to eat it with.*

Opposite right: **ROAST LEG OF LAMB WITH MUSTARD**
**HERB CRUST** *(page 61) served here with* **BAKED ONION**
**HALVES** *(page 45) and* **OLD FASHIONED MINT SAUCE**
*(page 65).*

# M A R I N A T E D   L A M B   L O I N S

*½ cup red wine*
*1 cup oil*
*2 tablespoons dried rosemary leaves*
*5 cloves garlic, crushed*
*12 well-trimmed lamb loins or lamb fillets*

Heat first four ingredients together in a small saucepan to make
the marinade, stirring until the mixture comes to the boil. Turn
off heat and allow to cool to room temperature. Strain out the
rosemary leaves and pour over the lamb loins. Cover and marinate
for at least 4 hours, preferably overnight.

Drain lamb, shaking off excess marinade, but reserving it to
baste while cooking. Grill, panfry or barbecue the lamb over high
heat — 2 minutes each side for rare or a little longer according
to taste, but don't overcook because loins and fillets are so tender
and juicy if pink, but can toughen and become chewy if overdone.

## P O R T   A N D   B L A C K B E R R Y   S A U C E

*250–300 g fresh or frozen blackberries (or*
   *substitute other berries)*
*¼ cup sugar or to taste*
*2 cups port*
*2 tablespoons arrowroot*
*¼ cup cold water*
*fresh rosemary sprigs to garnish*

Reserve a few berries to garnish and bring the rest to the boil
with sugar and port, then turn down heat and simmer for 10
minutes. Pour through a fine sieve to remove blackberry pips and
return to saucepan.

Mix arrowroot and cold water to a paste, then add 2 tablespoons
of the port and berry mixture. Return this to the saucepan, stirring
continuously over a gentle heat as the sauce clears and thickens.
If it's too thick, a little extra water or port may be stirred in.

To serve, ladle a spoonful of sauce on to a warm dinner plate
and serve the sliced lamb loin on the sauce, garnish with fresh
berries and a sprig of fresh rosemary.

***Serves 6***

# LAMB AND FETA CHEESE SALAD

*A boned leg of lamb, roasted or grilled lamb loins or fillets are all good cuts of lamb to use. This is a meal and salad all in one go, and travels well to a picnic or out sailing etc.*

500 g rare-cooked cold lamb, cut into bite-
  sized pieces
2 cups sliced or halved button mushrooms
2 red capsicums, cut into strips
250 g cherry tomatoes
6–8 zucchini, sliced and blanched
100 g Feta cheese, cut into small cubes
1 cup black olives (optional)
½ cup chopped chives or small spring onions

DRESSING

5 tablespoons olive or salad oil
2 tablespoons white wine vinegar
2 cloves garlic, crushed
2 tablespoons chopped fresh basil
2 tablespoons chopped parsley

Make dressing first by mixing all ingredients in a blender or food processor until well combined.

Carefully toss salad ingredients in dressing and serve ungarnished on a large platter.

**Serves 4**

## BARBECUED LAMB WITH SOUR CREAM AND FRESH HERBS

*250 g sour cream*
*4 cloves garlic, crushed*
*2 tablespoons chopped fresh parsley*
*1 teaspoon finely chopped fresh rosemary*
*1 teaspoon finely chopped fresh oregano*
*1 teaspoon finely chopped fresh thyme*
*1 teaspoon salt*
*1 teaspoon freshly ground black pepper*
*3 kg boned leg of lamb, trimmed and*
   *butterflied*
*fresh herbs to garnish*

Mix first eight ingredients to make marinade and spread over all surfaces of the lamb. Cover, chill and marinate for at least 4 hours, preferably overnight.

Bring to room temperature before cooking. Barbecue or grill to desired level of doneness. Allow the lamb to rest at room temperature for 10 minutes, then slice thinly across the grain. Serve as a main dish with salad or vegetable accompaniments, or as slices on salad leaves with a vinaigrette dressing. Garnish with fresh herbs.

**Serves 4–6**

## CORIANDER LAMB SATAYS

*150 ml red wine*
*1 tablespoon lemon juice*
*200 ml oil*
*2 cloves garlic, crushed*
*1 tablespoon finely chopped fresh coriander*
*freshly ground black pepper to taste*
*500 g lean lamb strips cut from loin, fillet or*
   *shoulder*
*fresh coriander sprigs to garnish*

Mix first six ingredients in blender or food processor to make marinade. Marinate meat for 3–4 hours or overnight. Drain marinade, reserving to use as a baste while grilling.

Thread strips of lamb on to metal or soaked bamboo skewers and cook over a high heat for approximately 3–5 minutes, turning frequently and basting with the marinade.

Serve satays on rice with coriander to garnish, and Coriander and Mint Sauce alongside for dipping satays in.

### CORIANDER AND MINT SAUCE

*1 cup natural yoghurt*
*2 tablespoons finely chopped coriander*
*2 tablespoons finely chopped mint leaves*
*1 tablespoon liquid honey*
*salt and freshly ground black pepper*
*1 clove garlic, crushed*
*½ teaspoon sweet chilli sauce or few drops*
   *Tabasco sauce*

Thoroughly mix all ingredients and chill for 2–3 hours for flavours to develop.

**Serves 4**

# LAMB CUTLETS WITH MINT JULEP SAUCE

*The number of lamb cutlets depends on their size. Some cutlets are very tiny and you may want to serve more.*

6 lamb cutlets
½ cup finely chopped mint
¼ cup white wine vinegar
½ cup sugar
¼ cup bourbon
1 tablespoon arrowroot
¼ cup cold water
mint sprigs to garnish

Cook the lamb over a high heat, either panfrying, grilling, or barbecuing, brushing with a little oil to prevent it sticking. I cook it for 2 minutes each side but you may like it a teeny bit longer for medium rare. However, these cuts must be served pink as they can become very chewy and tough if overdone.

To make the sauce, in a small saucepan stir mint, vinegar, sugar and bourbon over a gentle heat. Bring to the boil then reduce heat. Mix arrowroot with cold water and add 2 tablespoons of the mint mixture and stir well. Return to saucepan, stirring as it clears and thickens. Don't allow sauce to boil.

Serve the lamb cutlets on sauce and garnish with mint.

**Serves 6**

# OLD-FASHIONED MINT SAUCE FOR ROAST LAMB

1 cup mint leaves
2 teaspoons sugar
2 tablespoons malt vinegar
¼ cup boiling water

Carefully remove any stalks and less-than-perfect mint leaves and wash and shake dry. Sprinkle with the sugar and chop finely. (My Granny's old mint sauce mincer is purpose-built for this job, so lucky you if you can find one, too.)

Place chopped leaves in a small bowl and pour vinegar and water over. Allow to cool before serving as this really brings out the flavour.

**Makes about ½ cup**

## BEEF

*Generally beef prices in New Zealand are higher than those of lamb so it's more of a special treat. Our mostly British origins are probably the main reason that we, as a country, love our beef — whether it is the classic Olde English roast beef and Yorkshire pudding, a Sunday roast dinner or the modern New Zealand barbecue steak.*

*Beef should always be cooked rare when roasted or grilled but slow-simmered aromatic stews and casseroles, where the meat melts in your mouth, certainly have a place of importance in my culinary routine.*

**STUFFED RIB-EYE FILLET STEAK WITH SOUR CREAM MUSTARD SAUCE.**

# STUFFED RIB-EYE FILLET STEAK

*For this dish, have the butcher cut you a prime piece of rib-eye fillet, trimmed of all sinews and membranes, with the meat being the same thickness all along the fillet (i.e. cutting off the thick end and tail end).*

*I have always found that 20 minutes on high heat works perfectly for the beef to make it rare pink, but not too underdone. Try it this way first before adding or deducting cooking time to suit your taste.*

*1 trimmed rib-eye fillet*
*3 tablespoons whole-grain mustard*
*10 spinach leaves, washed and steamed or cooked for a minute in the microwave to wilt*
*salt and freshly ground black pepper*

Preheat oven to 220°C. Make a 1 cm-deep slice in the fillet lengthways and carefully cut it open, peeling the meat back as though you were unrolling a Swiss roll, so you end up with a flattened rectangle of meat.

Spread this generously with the mustard and lay the wilted spinach leaves over. Carefully roll meat back into its original shape, securing with natural fibre string (or dental floss perhaps, not the mint-flavoured one). Sprinkle with salt and a generous amount of pepper.

Cook in preheated oven for a timed 20 minutes — no longer. This will result in gorgeous pink medium-rare meat, which is how it should be, juicy and melt-in-the-mouth. Allow meat to sit for 5 minutes before removing string and slicing.

**Variations:**
My favourite fillings are:

• oysters for a version of the classic carpet bag steak
• capers and French-style mustard
• garlic, mushrooms and pine nuts
• fresh snipped herbs, spring onions and chives

## SOUR CREAM MUSTARD SAUCE

*150 g tub sour cream*
*3 tablespoons whole-grain mustard*
*1 tablespoon chopped parsley*
*salt and freshly ground black pepper*

To make the sauce, mix the sour cream, mustard and parsley thoroughly, adding salt and pepper to taste. There is no need to heat this: just have it at room temperature.

Serve on warmed dinner plates, two to three slices of beef per person, and pour the sauce over the top — the heat of the meat is enough to gently warm it through.

**Serves 4**

# FARMHOUSE CORNED SILVERSIDE

*Here is a little bit of England — a tribute to my British heritage. Corned beef dinners are just as popular here in New Zealand but they just aren't the same without the sauce.*

1 piece corned silverside, approximately
   2.5 kg
2 tablespoons malt vinegar
2 tablespoons brown sugar
6 peppercorns
6 cloves
1 onion, roughly chopped
2 bay leaves

Place corned silverside in a large saucepan, cover with cold water and add remaining ingredients. Cover and bring to a gentle simmer. Cook for 2½–3 hours until the meat is just tender.

## MUSTARD SAUCE

½ cup strained liquid the meat has
   cooked in
½ cup malt vinegar
1 tablespoon mustard powder
1 tablespoon flour
2 eggs

Mix all ingredients thoroughly together with a wire whisk, stir over a very gentle heat until it thickens. Thin if necessary with a little extra corned beef liquid.

The liquid can also be used to cook small potatoes and carrots, the classic accompaniment to corned beef. Finely shredded cabbage, sautéed in a little butter and the corned beef liquid, is the second accompaniment.

Leftover silverside is delicious the next day, eaten cold, or you could slice it thinly and combine it with small button mushrooms, sliced spring onions, and any leftover Mustard Sauce plus a little cream. Toss this combination together with hot pasta and you've got an instant gourmet dinner.

**Serves 4–6**

# SHEARERS' RICH BEEF CASSEROLE WITH FIELD MUSHROOMS

*5 rashers bacon, chopped*
*2 medium-sized onions, sliced*
*4 cloves garlic, crushed*
*50 g butter*
*1.5 kg chuck steak cut into chunky pieces*
*2 tablespoons flour*
*1 cup port or red wine*
*1 cup beef stock, or 1 teaspoon beef stock*
  *powder dissolved in 1 cup water*
*2 tablespoons tomato paste or purée*
*1 teaspoon mixed dried herbs, rosemary,*
  *thyme, sage, etc. or 1 tablespoon chopped*
  *fresh herbs*
*1 stick celery, sliced*
*6–8 small carrots, scrubbed*
*250 g field mushrooms, sliced*
*chopped parsley*
*salt and freshly ground black pepper to taste*
*chopped fresh parsley to garnish*

Fry chopped bacon slowly in a large frypan, extracting as much fat as possible. Remove bacon to a large ovenware casserole, leaving fat in frypan. Fry onion and garlic in bacon fat for 5–6 minutes then remove to casserole dish. Add butter to frying pan. Dust steak pieces in flour and brown in the butter. Add meat to casserole dish. Swill out pan with the port or red wine, beef stock or water and stock. Add the tomato paste and stir to include all the meat juices and pan scrapings. Pour into casserole. Add herbs, celery and carrots, sliced mushrooms and salt and pepper to taste.

Place lid on casserole and cook in a slow oven, 150°C, for 3 hours or until meat is really tender. Stir every now and then and to serve, garnish with extra chopped parsley. Serve with baked potatoes and lots of crusty bread to mop up all the delicious gravy.

**Serves 6–8**

# YORKSHIRE PUDDING

*1½ cups flour*
*1 teaspoon salt*
*4 eggs*
*1½ cups milk*
*1 tablespoon cold water*
*pan drippings from roast beef*

Sift flour and salt into a bowl. Gradually beat in eggs and milk, stir in cold water.

Remove roast beef from oven, and allow it to rest before carving. Pour 2 teaspoons of pan drippings into each of 12 deep muffin tins, or pour 3–4 tablespoons of dripping into a deep ovenproof dish or loaf pan. Increase oven temperature to 220°C, and place muffin tins or dish in oven until dripping begins to smoke. Pour in batter, filling tins or pan three-quarters full. Bake in hot oven for 20–30 minutes, or until puffed and golden brown. Serve the pudding as soon as it comes from the oven, as an accompaniment to roast beef.

**Makes 12**

*Mother's good old home-made meat loaf is taken to new gastronomic heights in its guise as* **SAGE MEAT LOAF WITH MUSTARD CREAM SAUCE.** *The loaf is equally delicious when eaten cold and it makes a great sandwich filling, too.*

# SAGE MEAT LOAF

*1.5 kg lean prime beef mince*
*1½ cups coarse fresh breadcrumbs*
*1 cup tomato sauce*
*2 eggs*
*⅓ cup finely grated Parmesan cheese*
*2 tablespoons chopped, fresh parsley*
*2 tablespoons chopped capers*
*1 teaspoon salt*
*½ teaspoon freshly ground black pepper*
*2 tablespoons oil*
*1 medium-sized onion, finely chopped*
*3 cloves garlic, crushed*
*¼ cup finely chopped green capsicum*
*¼ cup finely chopped fresh sage or*
   *1–1½ teaspoons dried*
*2 teaspoons finely chopped fresh sweet*
   *marjoram*
*½ teaspoon finely chopped fresh lemon thyme*

Preheat oven to 180°C. In a large bowl combine minced beef, breadcrumbs, tomato sauce, eggs, Parmesan cheese, parsley, capers, salt and pepper. In a heavy medium-sized frypan, warm oil over a low heat. Add onion, garlic and capsicum and cook until onion is golden — about 5 minutes. Add sage, marjoram and lemon thyme and cook over a low heat for 1 minute, then add to ingredients in the bowl. Using your hands, thoroughly mix meat loaf ingredients.

Pack meat firmly into a well-greased loaf pan, mounding slightly in the middle. Bake meat loaf for about 1½ hours or until it has pulled away from the sides of the pan, is nicely browned and firm to touch. Allow to cool in the pan on a rack for 15 minutes.

## MUSTARD CREAM SAUCE

*½ cup whole-grain mustard*
*2 teaspoons cornflour, stirred into ¼ cup*
   *water*
*150 ml cream or sour cream*
*1 tablespoon chopped parsley*

Stir all ingredients together over a low heat until blended and thickened. Pour over meat loaf slices and garnish with sage leaves.

**Serves 4–6**

### H A N G I

*A hangi (steaming food on hot stones in a subterranean oven) is a very popular way for New Zealanders to have a big 'cookout' when friends are gathered together. It's a happy blend of the traditional Maori way of cooking with innovations and additions provided by Pakeha neighbours. The version our family often uses is not dissimilar to a New England clambake.*

*The site selection is important and should depend on access to water in which to soak sacks to create the necessary steam. Consider also how hard it will be to dig the pit, wind direction and the general ambience of the site so guests can eat without discomfort and in pleasant surroundings. We have a perfect 'possie' down by the creek on the farm with lots of good, dense, even-sized river boulders. There's plenty of available manuka firewood, with the stream running by and a natural setting with rocks to sit on and ferns to shade us. The stones are very important and should ideally be porous volcanic rock, or dense river stones that don't crack and heat easily. I've been to some good hangis that have used lumps of railway iron or even fire bricks in the absence of good stones.*

*All types of food — fish and shellfish, chicken, red meats and, of course, kumara and vegetables — can be successfully cooked hangi-fashion. We wrap well-seasoned chicken portions in tinfoil, leave shellfish in their shells, and crayfish and fish whole. If possible, we bone out butterflied joints of meat for quicker cooking, or give larger cuts a bit of time in the domestic oven first. Large, uncooked joints of meat take 4–5 hours in the hangi, which would be far too long for the other foods. Sometimes we even cook a couple of steamed puds in with the hangi.*

*The food should be ready after about 2–2½ hours. There's some guesswork involved but this should be long enough. Carefully dig out the hangi and enjoy the gorgeous aromas that waft out to meet you.*

*I always serve lots of crispy salads and have dressings and dipping sauces of butter at the ready, especially for the seafood and chicken, which, although juicy and moist cooked hangi-fashion, often needs a little vamping up to enhance the slightly smoky flavour. Lots of marinades and herbs used in the food preparation also help with flavours. Have a good supply of rock salt and freshly ground black pepper on hand, too.*

## GLAZED HAM

*These days most people buy their Christmas ham precooked. Making your own glaze is simple and the end result looks quite stunning, especially if you decorate the bone with a ribbon or a paper frill and use the ham as the centrepiece for a festive buffet dinner.*

### BOURBON HONEY GLAZE

½ cup liquid honey
2 teaspoons French mustard
½ cup bourbon
3 cloves

Carefully peel back the leathery skin from the precooked leg of ham on the bone. Slide your hands underneath the skin to help ease it away from the layer of fat underneath. Discard skin. Using a sharp knife, score the surface of the ham with a diamond pattern.

Gently heat ingredients for glaze in a small saucepan and simmer for 10 minutes. Remove cloves and brush skinned ham with desired glaze. Bake ham in a medium hot oven, 170–180°C, for 45–60 minutes, basting frequently until the surface is a rich golden brown.

Serve warm or at room temperature. Use the bone as a handle to assist with carving.

## HONEY-GLAZED PORK FILLETS

3 cloves garlic, crushed
3 tablespoons tomato sauce
¼ cup light soya sauce
4 tablespoons liquid honey
4 pork fillets

In a food processor or blender, thoroughly mix the garlic, tomato sauce, soya sauce and honey. Marinate pork fillets in this mixture for 2 hours, turning to evenly coat with the marinade.

Bake pork on a wire rack over a baking dish for 30–35 minutes in a hot oven, 200°C, basting with remaining marinade.

**Serves 4**

## CHICKEN

*Chicken, until quite recently, was regarded as a specialty meat for high days and holidays. In the later 1960s and early 1970s large-scale chicken farming was established where birds were bred especially for eating. Prices dropped accordingly and chicken today is one of the cheapest meats, readily available in an interesting variety of cuts and portions.*

# CHICKEN BREASTS WRAPPED IN BACON

*These are very simple to prepare but look spectacular and will have your guests complimenting you on your advanced culinary skills.*

6 single boneless chicken breasts
6 rashers bacon, rindless
½ teaspoon Cajun Seasoning Mix

Wrap each breast, skin side up, with a bacon rasher, in a figure-eight pattern. Sprinkle with the Cajun Seasoning Mix and bake at 180°C for approximately 20 minutes until the bacon is crisp and the chicken breast cooked through. Serve with vegetables or a salad of your choice and perhaps a very simple mustard, salsa or chutney accompaniment.

### Variation:

Insert a few capers inside the chicken breast and secure with the bacon rasher. Serve with Caper Grainy Mustard Sauce.

## CAPER GRAINY MUSTARD SAUCE

100 g butter
3 tablespoons flour
1½ cups milk
1 tablespoon grainy mustard
1 tablespoon chopped parsley
3 tablespoons capers, drained
salt and freshly ground black pepper to taste

Melt butter in a small saucepan or in the microwave. Stir in the flour and cook for a few minutes. Add the milk, slowly whisking with a wire whisk as the sauce thickens. Add the mustard, parsley and capers. Add extra milk if a thinner consistency is required. Taste the sauce and adjust the seasoning with salt and pepper to your liking. Spoon over the cooked crispy chicken breasts.

**Serves 6**

*PERSIAN CHICKEN is best served with a rice dish to soak up all the wonderful juices. It's also a useful recipe to have in your repertoire because the flavours are just as good when it's served cold.*

# PERSIAN CHICKEN

*This is a recipe I use a lot when I'm entertaining. I do hot and cold versions and use it as a base for other variations such as chicken wrapped in phyllo pastry with apricots and served with this sauce.*

2 large onions
1 cup water
1 cup red wine
2 teaspoons chicken stock powder
1 tablespoon curry powder
3 tablespoons tomato purée
1 kg cooked chicken meat
250 g small button mushrooms
3 spring onions, finely sliced
1 cup of grapes, green or black
400 g can apricots, drained and sliced
½ cup coarsely chopped parsley
½ cup prepared mayonnaise
1 cup cream, lightly whipped

Roughly chop the onions and place in a large heavy-bottomed saucepan or casserole. Add the water, wine, chicken stock powder, curry powder and tomato purée. Simmer for 30 minutes until liquid has reduced and mixture has a chutney-like appearance. Stir frequently during cooking time.

Add diced chicken meat, washed whole mushrooms, spring onions, grapes and apricots. Cook for about 5 minutes to warm chicken through, then fold in parsley, mayonnaise and cream. Serve immediately. This is great with rice or noodles and a crisp salad, but is also very good cold, as a spicy chicken salad.

**Variation:**

Try replacing the apricots with fresh feijoas or nectarine slices and using melon instead of grapes for a creamy chicken salad.

*Serves 6–8*

# G A R L I C   R O S E M A R Y   C H I C K E N

6 single boneless chicken breasts with skin
    removed
½ cup red wine
1 cup oil
2 tablespoons dried rosemary leaves
5 cloves of garlic, crushed

Put all ingredients except chicken in a small saucepan, stirring until it comes to the boil. Turn off heat and allow to cool to room temperature. Strain out rosemary leaves and pour over chicken breasts. Cover and marinate for 2–4 hours.

Barbecue, panfry or grill chicken over a high heat until cooked through and golden brown, about 6–7 minutes each side, depending on thickness of breasts. Serve with sweetcorn fritters and grilled tomatoes.

**Serves 6**

# T R O P I C A L   C H I C K E N   W I T H   P A W P A W   A N D   G R A P E S

1 large onion, roughly chopped
1 tablespoon tomato purée
2 teaspoons curry powder
1 cup chicken stock
1 cup red wine
1½ cups mayonnaise
300 ml cream, thickly whipped
3–4 cups chicken, cooked and sliced
large bunch grapes
4–6 slices fresh pawpaw, 2 tablespoons
    parsley, roughly chopped, and 2–3 chive
    flowers to garnish

Simmer chopped onion, tomato purée, curry powder, chicken stock and red wine for 30 minutes until well reduced to a chutney-like consistency. When cold fold in the mayonnaise and cream. Mix in the chicken and grapes, and spoon on to a large serving platter. Garnish with slices of pawpaw and sprinkle with chopped parsley and the petals of chive flowers. You can add to the garnishes with fresh tropical flowers — such as hibiscus, passionflowers and frangipani.

**Serves 4–6**

**TROPICAL CHICKEN WITH PAWPAW AND GRAPES** *lends itself well to attractive presentation on a large platter with a garnish of extra tropical fruits and flowers.*

## F R I E D   L E M O N   C H I C K E N   W I T H   S E S A M E   S E E D S

1½ cups milk
juice of 2 large lemons, and zest of 2 large
  lemons, separated
8 single boneless chicken breasts with skin
  removed
2 tablespoons coarse ground cornmeal
2 tablespoons flour
2 tablespoons sesame seeds
1 teaspoon salt
freshly ground black pepper to taste
50 g butter
¼ cup oil
extra flour for sauce
¾ cup chicken stock
1 teaspoon finely chopped fresh lemon thyme
¾ cup cream
1 tablespoon chopped parsley

In a bowl combine milk and lemon juice. Marinate chicken in this for 2 hours, turning a couple of times.

In a separate shallow dish, combine cornmeal, flour, sesame seeds, lemon zest, salt and pepper.

Remove chicken from the milk. Do not pat dry but dredge in the cornmeal mixture to coat completely.

Heat the butter and oil in a large frypan over a medium to high heat. Fry the chicken until golden brown, turning at least once for about 8–10 minutes. Transfer to a warmed serving platter.

Stir 1 teaspoon flour into frypan scrapings. Stir in the chicken stock and thyme and simmer, scraping up all browned bits in the pan. Add the cream and parsley and a squeeze of extra lemon juice. Cook for 2–3 minutes until thickened slightly. Season to taste and serve with the chicken.

**Serves 4–6**

## C H I C K E N   B R E A S T S   W I T H   G A R L I C   A N D   T O M A T O E S

3 tablespoons olive oil
4 single chicken breasts with bones intact
4 medium-sized tomatoes, chopped
10 large garlic cloves, peeled
3 tablespoons white wine or vermouth
2 sprigs fresh oregano (or ½ teaspoon dried
  oregano)
salt and freshly ground black pepper to taste
extra fresh herbs to garnish

*Don't be put off the by the number of garlic cloves in this recipe. They become sweet and mild-tasting when cooked slowly.*

Heat oil in a large frypan over a medium heat. Add chicken and cook for 3–5 minutes on each side, or until golden brown. Lower heat and add tomatoes, garlic, wine and oregano. Season with salt and pepper. Cover and simmer for 15 minutes. Mash tomatoes lightly with a fork. Garnish with fresh herbs.

**Serves 4**

# CHICKEN BLUEBIRDS

4 single boneless chicken breasts, (skinned if
   desired)
3 tablespoons flour for dusting
oil for frying
100 g butter
1 tablespoon flour
1½ cups milk
100 g blue vein cheese
1 tablespoon chopped fresh herbs such as
   parsley, chives and chervil, etc.
1 teaspoon cracked white peppercorns to
   garnish

Dust chicken breasts with flour and very gently sauté in oil until golden brown.

Melt the butter in a small saucepan or in the microwave and stir in next measure of flour. Add milk slowly, whisking sauce as it thickens. Crumble two-thirds of the cheese into sauce and add the herbs. Mix until smooth and well blended. To serve, pour sauce over chicken breasts, sprinkle with remaining blue cheese and a few cracked white peppercorns.

**Serves 4**

# TURKEY PHYLLO BON-BONS WITH CRANBERRY PORT SAUCE

12 sheets phyllo pastry
1 double turkey breast fillet, divided into
   6 portions
3 teaspoons Cajun Seasoning Mix
100 g butter, melted
holly leaf or sprig of rosemary to garnish

Preheat oven to 180°C. Fold 2 sheets of phyllo pastry in half. Place a portion of turkey fillet on the phyllo pastry, sprinkle with ½ teaspoon Cajun Seasoning Mix and roll up like a Christmas cracker or bon-bon, pinching the ends of the pastry together. Brush generously with melted butter and place on a greased or non-stick baking tray. Keep chilled in the refrigerator until ready to cook. They can be frozen at this stage.

Bake bon-bons for 15–20 minutes until pastry is golden and crispy. Check that the turkey has cooked through by inserting a sharp knife into the underside of 1 bon-bon, making a tiny peep-hole. Reduce heat and cook a few minutes longer if the turkey filling is still a little underdone. The cooking time depends on the size of the phyllo parcel.

Serve on a little pool of Cranberry Port Sauce and garnish with a holly leaf or sprig of rosemary.

## CRANBERRY PORT SAUCE

This is a really easy sauce as all you need to do is stir together ¼ cup port and a 250 g can whole cranberry sauce. Heat the combination gently over a medium heat before serving.

## G A M E

*Short open shooting seasons, with strict controls, have ensured stable populations of all varieties of game birds in New Zealand.*

*Wild ducks should be hung for 2–3 days in a dry, well-ventilated place, before plucking and drawing. By then they should have a distinctive gamy flavour, without being really 'high'. Plump or smaller birds are best for roasting, while large ducks, or ducks of doubtful age, are best casseroled, or reserved for soup and pâté making.*

*The distinctive gamy flavour of wild fowl is desirable although for lots of people there is a fine line between 'gamy' and 'off'. I am personally not particularly good at plucking and gutting wild ducks and swan etc. but, if someone deals with all that, I am very happy to cook the finished and cleaned product. I generally opt for long slow simmering with lots of wine and aromatic herbs for duck as the age of the bird is guess-work. Slow cooking generally ensures tenderness and you can always make a good soup or pâté if all else fails.*

*Wild venison is still a fairly rare treat even with the advent of commercial deer farms. Wild venison should be hung properly before eating and the flavour and texture is really enhanced by maturing.*

*Wild pork meat is much darker and stronger than domestic pork and the flavour can vary considerably, depending on what food the pig has been living on. Most wild pork is greatly improved by hanging properly before cooking.*

**ROAST WILD DUCK** — *you can substitute a frozen or farmed duck if you're not lucky enough to have access to the real thing and it will still be delicious.*

# R O A S T   W I L D   D U C K

2×1.5 kg wild ducks
50 g butter, melted
2 tablespoons oil
salt and freshly ground black pepper

Mix the melted butter and oil and brush ducks liberally. Roast at 200°C for an hour. Reduce heat to 180°C and turn ducks over, cooking for a further 30 minutes, or until tender. During cooking, baste frequently with the pan juices. When cooked remove ducks from roasting dish. Pour off fat. Keep ducks warm while making sauce.

## H O N E Y E D   T A M A R I L L O   R E D   W I N E   S A U C E

8 tamarillos, peeled and sliced
1 cup red wine
¼ cup liquid honey
juice and zest of 1 medium-sized lemon
1 tablespoon arrowroot
½ cup cold water
fresh herbs and extra tamarillo slices to
    garnish

In a small saucepan bring the tamarillo slices, red wine and honey to the boil. Turn down heat and allow to simmer for 3–4 minutes. Add the lemon juice and zest. Mix the arrowroot and cold water together in a cup and add 3 tablespoons of the hot tamarillo wine liquid. Pour back into the saucepan, stirring constantly, until the sauce thickens and clears.

When the ducks are cooked, carve and place portions on a serving dish. Spoon over sauce and garnish with herbs and extra tamarillo.

***Serves 4***

# WILD DUCK WITH APPLES AND CIDER

2 × 700 g ducks
100 g butter, melted
salt and freshly ground black pepper to taste
1.5 litres dry cider
1 teaspoon chopped fresh thyme or lemon
    thyme
150 ml cream
1 kg tart cooking apples, peeled and
    quartered
fresh herb sprigs to garnish

Brush ducks with melted butter. Season with salt and pepper and roast in a hot oven, 220°C, for 45 minutes until browned. Remove from oven and pour cider over. Cook for a few more minutes then remove ducks from roasting pan and keep warm.

Stir thyme into pan and reduce the sauce by half. Stir in cream and reduce again by about a third. Return ducks to the roasting dish, ladling sauce over them. Surround them with the apples and cook for a further 10–15 minutes until apples are tender. Adjust the seasoning of the sauce if required.

Place ducks on a serving dish and surround with the apples. Pour over sauce and garnish with sprigs of fresh herbs.

**Serves 4–6**

# FEIJOA SALSA

*A great side dish to serve with roast wild duck. And feijoas and duck shooting are both in season in May. You can also serve this salsa with plain grilled chicken or steak.*

10–12 feijoas, roughly chopped
grated zest and juice of 4 lemons or limes
2 spring onions, very finely chopped
2 teaspoons sweet chilli sauce or finely
    chopped fresh chilli to taste
4 medium-sized tomatoes, peeled, deseeded
    and chopped
1 tablespoon balsamic vinegar
2 tablespoons chopped parsley
¼ cup oil
salt and freshly ground black pepper to taste

Mix everything together. Cover and chill for at least 1 hour and preferably up to 3 hours. Stir just before serving.

**Makes about 1½ cups**

# STIR-FRY VENISON WITH PICKLED WALNUTS

500 g venison topside or rump, trimmed
¼ cup chilli vinegar
½ cup walnut oil
5 spring onions, finely sliced
2 small onions, sliced into rings
15–20 fine green beans, sliced
1 teaspoon fresh finely chopped ginger
1 teaspoon sweet chilli sauce
6 pickled walnuts, drained and sliced
1 punnet snow pea shoots

Remove all sinew and membrane from meat and cut into long finger-like strips.

Combine meat, chilli vinegar and walnut oil. Leave to marinate for 2 hours.

Over a high heat, stir-fry meat in a wok until browned (this may have to be done in batches). Remove meat and stir-fry spring onions, onion rings and beans. Add ginger and chilli sauce. Lastly return meat to wok and add pickled walnuts and snow pea shoots. Toss to warm through and serve immediately. Serve with rice.

***Serves 4***

# GRILLED VENISON WITH HOT MUSTARD DRESSING

1 kg venison striploin
a little oil
4 tablespoons grainy mustard
2 tablespoons white wine vinegar
1 tablespoon Colman's hot English mustard
    powder
125 g sour cream
1 tablespoon chopped parsley

Cut venison striploin into 2 cm thick slices. Brush all surfaces with the oil and grill or barbecue over a high heat for 2 minutes each side. Combine all other ingredients in a small saucepan and heat gently or microwave in a bowl. Stir with a wire whisk until well combined. Serve meat with dressing poured over it and accompany with a crisp, green salad.

***Serves 4–6***

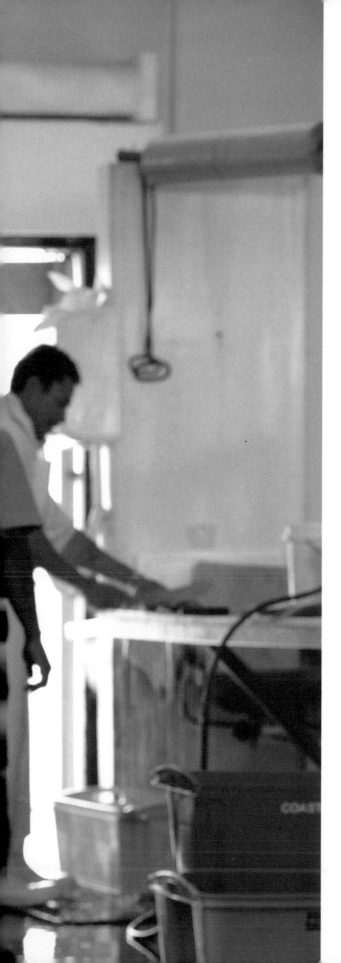

# F I S H

I grew up with a great love for fishing. My first catches were restricted to sprats and similar small-fry but these days I love to go trout fishing and, when time allows, out on game-fishing expeditions. There's something about catching your own food that makes it taste extra special.

New Zealand's remote and pollution-free environment is home to an amazing diversity of fish species ranging from subtropical to sub-antarctic varieties. There are over 80 commercially fished types with a total allowable catch of 600,000 tonnes annually. Fish is low in fat and calories, packed full of protein and minerals and it's a real boon for cooks in a hurry. It tastes good, too. Because, let's face it, if it didn't — no amount of health and consumer information could persuade people of its other virtues.

We haven't always been a traditional fish-eating nation but things are changing — now, there's such a variety of seafood available it's possible to eat it practically every night without ever becoming bored. My fish philosophy is to buy as fresh as possible and cook speedily. Things to look for when you're buying whole fish are clear eyes and a fresh smell. The fresh smell also applies to fillets and you should look carefully at their texture.

# F I S H   F R I E D   I N   C R I S P Y   B E E R   B A T T E R

*2 cups flour*
*½ teaspoon salt*
*2 tablespoons butter, melted*
*120 ml beer*
*1 cup lukewarm water*
*2 large egg whites, stiffly beaten*
*oil for frying*
*1 kg firm white fish fillets, cut into strips*
*lemon wedges*

To make batter, sift flour and salt into a large mixing bowl, make a well in the centre, add melted butter, beer and water. Whisk together until batter is smooth, then cover bowl and let stand in a warm place for 1 hour. Just before using, fold in the beaten egg white.

Heat oil to 190°C. Dry fish pieces on paper towels, dip into batter and fry for about 2–3 minutes on each side in small batches. Drain on paper towels, keeping each batch warm in the oven until all are cooked. Serve with lemon wedges for squeezing.

***Serves 4–6***

## C O A T I N G S   F O R   P A N F R I E D   F I S H   F I L L E T S

Nothing could be simpler than merely dusting fabulously fresh fish fillets with flour, panfrying in a little butter or oil and serving with lemon wedges. However, I enjoy experimenting with different coatings and batters to extend my repertoire of tasty fish dishes.

Another basic coating is made by dipping fish in beaten egg then breadcrumbs. You can carry on this simple theme by adding interesting titbits and flavours to the crumbs. Sesame seeds are great for both flavour and texture, and particularly nice if you cook the fish in a mixture of butter and sesame oil. Grated citrus zest — lemon, orange or lime — can be added to the crumbs, and the citrus juice can be combined with the pan scrapings for a quick sauce. Chilli powder or cayenne pepper in the crumbs adds a zing, and you can replace the crumbs with oatmeal, buckwheat or cornmeal, or even ground nuts.

For really quick and easy sauces for fish, I use flavoured butters — the blender or food processor makes short work of this job. Some good combinations with butter are:

- lemon pepper, grated lemon zest
- fresh tarragon
- pine nut pesto
- sorrel or watercress
- mustard or horseradish
- pistachio, pecan, cashew or hazelnut with lots of freshly ground black pepper.

# FRESH SNAPPER FILLETS WITH BASIL CREAM SAUCE

*100 g butter*
*¼ cup finely chopped fresh basil*
*¼ cup dry white wine*
*2 cups good-flavoured fish stock*
*1 cup cream*
*salt to taste*
*½ teaspoon finely ground white pepper*
*6 medium-sized snapper fillets*
*flour to dust*
*oil for frying*
*fresh basil leaves and lemon slices to garnish*

Melt butter in a heavy frypan over a medium heat. Add basil and stir until wilted, about 1 minute. Add wine and stock and increase heat and boil until reduced by half (about 3–4 minutes). Add the cream and salt and pepper. Boil until the sauce is reduced to ¾ cup, about 8–10 minutes.

Wash and dry snapper fillets, lightly dust with flour and panfry in a little oil over a medium heat, 3–4 minutes each side. Keep warm if cooking in batches.

To serve, I like to spoon 2–3 tablespoons of sauce in the centre of each plate, tilting the plate to spread it evenly, then place the fish fillet in the centre, garnished with a fresh basil leaf or sprig, and some lemon slices or wedges.

Note: Sorrel or watercress is equally good in the sauce as a substitute for the fresh basil. Dried herbs just don't work the same in this recipe.

**Serves 4–6**

# PAWPAW CORIANDER SALSA

*1 small pawpaw or papaya, halved, seeded*
*   and coarsely chopped*
*2 teaspoons sweet chilli sauce, or finely*
*   chopped fresh chilli to taste*
*1 small red onion, peeled and finely chopped*
*2 tablespoons finely chopped fresh coriander*
*3 tablespoons fresh lemon or lime juice*
*2 tablespoons olive oil*
*salt and freshly ground black pepper to taste*

Mix everything together, cover and chill for at least 1 hour and up to 3 hours. Stir just before serving.

Serve with plain barbecued, grilled or panfried fish.

**Makes about 2 cups**

# GRILLED HAPUKA STEAKS WITH HAZELNUT LIME BUTTER

*Flavoured butters, especially with the addition of crunchy toasted nuts, are just perfect with grilled or panfried fish — either steaks, whole fish or fillets. They are especially good with chargrilled and barbecued fish.*

4 hapuka steaks
¼ cup chopped hazelnuts (toasted, with skins rubbed off)
1 spring onion, finely sliced
1 tablespoon chopped parsley
100 g butter
grated zest and juice of 4 medium-sized limes (separated)
1 tablespoon oil
salt and freshly ground black pepper
toasted hazelnuts and lime wedges to garnish

Rinse the hapuka steaks in cold water and pat dry with paper towels.

To make butter, in a food processor combine nuts, spring onion, parsley, lime zest and butter. Process just enough to blend ingredients without puréeing the nuts. Roll butter into a log and chill, wrapped in cling film.

Combine lime juice and oil and use to baste the steaks as they grill on a mesh rack 10–12 cm from the hot coals, or in a baking dish 10–12 cm from a preheated oven grill. Baste frequently and cook for 8 minutes per 2 cm thickness, measured at its thickest part. Turn halfway through cooking time.

Season with salt and freshly ground black pepper to taste and top with hazelnut butter. Serve immediately, garnished with a few toasted nuts and lime wedges.

Note: To toast hazelnuts, place in a single layer in a shallow baking dish. Roast for 5–6 minutes at 180°C until browned. Cool slightly, then rub the nuts briskly in a clean tea towel or paper towel, to remove some of the skins. (It's not necessary to remove them all.)

Instead of hazelnuts, toasted pecans, pistachios, cashews, macadamias, etc. can be used and fresh oranges or lemons could easily replace the lime. Any herbs or seasonings can be added to the flavoured butter to invent your own combinations, for example pistachio with lime and watercress, or sweet chilli butter with lemon thyme.

**Serves 4**

GRILLED HAPUKA STEAKS WITH HAZELNUT LIME BUTTER.

# S A L M O N   S T E A K S

So easy to prepare and always quite spectacular, the flesh of salmon is beautifully pink and they barbecue, grill or panfry equally well. I use quite fierce heat and brush the fish well with oil to prevent sticking. I find the microwave is a great way to cook salmon or to finish off cooking salmon steaks that have first been seared on a barbecue grill. Cooking times, of course, depend on the denseness of the fish, but generally the steaks need 5–6 minutes each side. Marinating salmon steaks is also a good idea to add flavour and the oil helps to prevent sticking while grilling.

Serve salmon steaks with a flavoured butter or a sauce. A very easy sauce for fish can be made by mixing a small tub of sour cream (150 g) with 2 tablespoons of prepared piccalilli, chow-chow, turmeric-coloured pickle or relish. People always ask me for the recipe for this sauce, thinking it must be a long and complicated procedure, but what could be easier?

## S I M P L E   T A S T Y   M A R I N A D E

*1 cup oil*
*½ cup fresh lemon juice*
*1 tablespoon chopped fresh herbs such as*
*    parsley, coriander, oregano, dill*
*½ teaspoon chilli powder or chopped fresh*
*    chilli or Tabasco to taste*
*salt and freshly ground black pepper to taste*

Mix all ingredients together.

*We're very fortunate to have such good quality salmon freely available in New Zealand.* **SALMON STEAKS** *can add a touch of luxury to any barbecue.*

# SALMON STEAKS ON WILD RICE WITH LEMON SHRIMP BUTTER

*You can cook these salmon steaks inside, using a heavy-based frypan, or outside on the barbecue. The different rices in the Wild Rice dish should be cooked separately, well in advance, and the Lemon Shrimp Butter should also be prepared in advance as the salmon takes no time to cook.*

6 salmon steaks
oil for brushing
a little lemon or lime juice
salt and pepper

Rinse salmon steaks and dry with paper towels. Lightly brush each one with oil on both sides. Fry over a high heat for 2 minutes then turn and cook the other side for the same time or until the flesh is cooked through. Drizzle a little lemon juice over each steak then season to taste.

## WILD RICE

200 g butter
4 spring onions, finely sliced
2 or 3 cloves garlic, crushed
2 cups cooked black wild rice
1 cup cooked long grain rice
1 cup cooked brown rice
1 teaspoon lemon pepper
1 large red capsicum, finely chopped
½ cup toasted pine nuts
1 cup chopped parsley
2 cups cooked shrimps
salt and freshly ground black pepper

Melt butter in a large pan. Add spring onion and garlic and cook for 2 minutes until soft. Add the different rices, mix well and allow to gently heat through. Add lemon pepper, chopped red pepper and pine nuts, again mixing well. Just before serving, stir through parsley and shrimps and season to taste.

## LEMON SHRIMP BUTTER

250 g butter, softened
½ cup cooked shrimp
juice and zest of 2 medium-sized lemons
½ teaspoon lemon pepper
½ teaspoon dried thyme
1 tablespoon finely chopped parsley

Mix all ingredients together in a blender or food processor until the shrimps are finely chopped and everything is well blended. Spoon out on to a sheet of cling film and roll into a cylindrical shape. Chill in freezer until required.

Remove cling film and cut into six slices. Place each salmon steak on a bed of rice and top with prepared butter before serving. The butter will quickly melt and drizzle through the fish and rice.

**Serves 6**

# SAUTÉED SQUID WITH GARLIC, LEMON AND FRESH HERBS

*Squid is still regarded by many New Zealanders as good only for bait fish. It is slowly gaining popularity, especially with so many young New Zealand travellers returning from overseas, particularly from Mediterranean countries, where squid is considered a luxury.*

*This is a lovely first course, or by adding fresh, crusty bread and salad leaves, it can be a substantial main meal.*

1 kiwifruit to marinate
1 cup cold water
1.5 kg squid tubes, cut into strips or rings
100 g butter or ¼ cup olive oil
3 cloves garlic, crushed
juice and grated zest of 3 medium-sized
    lemons
2 tablespoons finely chopped mixed herbs (use
    a combination of tarragon, parsley, dill,
    fennel and chervil)
salt and freshly ground black pepper to taste
black olives and sliced red capsicum to garnish

Purée flesh of the kiwifruit with the cold water. Strain through a fine sieve to remove pulp and seeds. Toss the rinsed squid rings or strips in the kiwifruit and water and leave for 5 minutes. Drain and rinse the squid. (Left any longer, the enzyme action of the kiwifruit goes beyond softening the tough fibres.)

Heat a large pan or wok and add butter or oil and garlic, cook for 1 minute, then add the squid, lemon and herbs. Toss for 2 minutes until squid loses its opaque look. Remove from heat, season with salt and pepper, and serve immediately, garnished with black olives and slices of red capsicum.

**Serves 4–6**

# MUSSELS STEAMED IN WINE

1 cup fruity white wine
¼ cup sprigs fresh herbs such as parsley, dill,
    fennel, thyme or marjoram
2 cloves garlic, crushed
36 mussels, scrubbed and with beards
    removed
¼ cup cream
salt and freshly ground black pepper to taste

Place wine, herbs and garlic in an extra-large saucepan then pile in the mussels. Cover and cook over a medium heat for 7–10 minutes or until all the mussels have steamed open. Using a slotted spoon, transfer mussels to individual serving bowls discarding any that have not opened.

Strain juice to remove broken bits of shell, herb stalks and any little crabs which might have been trapped inside.

Return juice to pan and bring to the boil. Allow to reduce then stir in cream and seasonings. Spoon this sauce over the mussels and serve with crusty bread.

**Serves 4–6**

**BACON AND MUSSEL KEBABS WITH CHILLI HONEY GLAZE** *taste as good as they look. If you're in a hurry, you can dispense with using fresh mussels and buy them already marinated to save yourself some time.*

# BACON AND MUSSEL KEBABS WITH CHILLI HONEY GLAZE

20 mussels
10 bacon rashers with rinds removed and cut
  into 5 cm-long strips

Steam open mussels and remove from shells. Wrap each mussel in a strip of bacon and thread on to skewers, 3–5 on each skewer, depending on the length.

## CHILLI HONEY GLAZE

3 tablespoons clear honey
2 tablespoons tomato sauce
1 teaspoon Worcestershire sauce
½ teaspoon ground black pepper
1 teaspoon chilli sauce or a few drops of
  Tabasco to taste

In a bowl combine glaze ingredients and pour over the mussels. Allow to marinate for 3–4 hours or overnight in the refrigerator.

Remove kebabs from glaze and barbecue or grill until bacon is crisp. Brush with leftover glaze while cooking.

Serve on a bed of rice or pasta with crispy salad accompaniment.

***Serves 3–4***

## S C A L L O P S

*Scallops are my absolute favourite, the fresher the better, and no one cooks them like my good friend Greg the Plumber.*

*During the average week, Greg can be spotted zooming around town in the Darth Vader black van. It's hard to miss with its 'WC' number plates and a couple of loos and lengths of pipe strapped on the roofrack.*

*However, come the weekend, it's down tools and he and his family are off to sea in their beautiful state-of-the-art launch. I'm not going to mention the name of it or you'll be frantically rowing over either to see what's on the barbecue or requesting some assistance with a nautical plumbing emergency. And besides, we're not silly, the longer we can keep Greg a secret the more gorgeous seafood for us.*

## G R E G ' S ' S C O L L I E S '

First catch your scallops. Ideally this recipe should use shellfish no older than 10 minutes from the sea.

Mix up a little bowl of garlic butter — no accurate measurements here, just add as much garlic as you like. Remember this guy is a plumber and has no formal chef's training, so he's a little light on specifics.

Clean the scallops of the yucky black and brown bits, so only the orange and white parts remain. Give the scallop shells a good scrub in seawater and put two or three scallops in each. Place a small knob of garlic butter on each scallop (about a teaspoonful), add a couple of tablespoons of white wine and a good grind of black pepper.

Carefully place the shells on the barbecue grill and cook for a few minutes only. The scallop meat should just turn white and the butter melt into the wine — any longer and they can turn quite rubbery and shrink. Even when they're removed from the grill the liquid poaches them for a moment or so longer. Now you're in for a taste sensation. Eat, enjoy, and don't forget to drink the divine juice.

## CRAYFISH

*There is no better way to serve crayfish than absolutely plain, straight from the pot, with lots of melted butter, salt and freshly ground black pepper. Flavoured butters are good, too. I drown the crayfish in fresh water first then bring the water to the boil for about 15–20 minutes.*

*I'm not happy in restaurants with big tanks of crayfish from which you get to choose your dinner. There's something not right about being personally introduced to your food before eating it.*

# CRAYFISH AND AVOCADO SALAD

*Selection of crisp salad leaves, washed and dried*
*3 avocados, peeled and cut into wedges*
*2 crayfish, cooked, removed from shells and chilled*
*¾ cup Watercress Mayonnaise*
*sprigs of watercress to garnish*
*freshly ground black pepper*

Arrange salad leaves on individual plates and place several avocado wedges on each. Slice crayfish tails and distribute evenly among plates in a pleasing arrangement. Ladle a spoonful of Watercress Mayonnaise over each portion and garnish with watercress. Dust each salad generously with black pepper.

**Serves 6**

# WATERCRESS MAYONNAISE FOR CRAYFISH

*6 egg yolks*
*2 tablespoons water*
*1 cup safflower oil*
*2 tablespoons lemon juice*
*1 cup olive oil*
*1 cup finely chopped watercress*

Place egg yolks and water in a blender or food processor and run the machine for about 6 seconds. With motor still running, slowly trickle in the first cup of oil. When mixture is thick and creamy, add a tablespoon of lemon, then very slowly trickle in the second cup of oil. Add the remainder of the lemon juice and then the chopped watercress. Mix for a further 20 or so seconds to really purée in the watercress. Check flavour, as a little seasoning may be required, although the watercress is quite peppery. Serve with fresh cooked crayfish.

**Makes about 2 cups**

## T R O U T

*In a blue-green pool, way up a Lake Taupo tributary river gorge miles away from civilisation, a big fat speckly trout awaits his supper. He hugs the shelter of the rocks at the pool's edge, hovering and waiting, body swaying slightly in the current, just a shimmering shadow. Soon a tasty insect alights on the water upstream and floats down, tempting him; he rises lazily to meet it. Eyeing his prey, he hesitates only for a fraction of a second, then with a whip of his tail he propels himself towards the surface, snaps at the insect, flips sideways in a neat little splash and dives for the safety of the deep. He has made a fatal error of judgement.*

*Downstream, Jo Seagar — angler extraordinaire in her glamorous rubber waders — sees the fish strike. A flick of the rod and the hook of the fraudulent fly secures itself in the trout's mouth. A few minutes later, supper is sizzling in the pan. I'm the one really hooked — on fishing, that is. I'm a learner, but I've had a good teacher in my dear friend Cliff Fenwick and I'm learning to read the signs correctly. This quest to capture fish with artificial flies — bits of fur and feathers tied to hooks — is timeless. The scene I've just outlined has been taking place for centuries.*

*There is nothing more relaxing than flyfishing out in the clean air with the sounds of the burbling water. Many rivers and lakes, most notably Lake Taupo, are famous worldwide for their rainbow and brown trout.*

*The tradition of smoking trout in order to preserve it goes back a long way. Prehistoric man probably came upon the technique, more by accident than design, by hanging the fish in the same cave as the open fire. Today, with the scientific advances in methods of food storage and refrigeration, smoking is regarded more for the distinctive flavour it imparts than as a method of preservation. There are two types of smoking processes.*

*Cold smoking is done by smoking at a lower temperature so that the fish is left still raw. The heat from the smouldering wood is not high enough to cook the food, but simply gives it a wonderfully appetising smoky flavour. Some cold-smoked foods, like salmon and cheeses, can be eaten raw, whereas poultry, hams and sausages, etc. would need further cooking.*

*Hot smoking, or smoke roasting, is done over a high heat which produces food that is cooked and ready to eat. The outside surface of the food absorbs the smoky flavour and the heat penetrates and cooks the food right through. Hot smoking the catch after a fishing trip, for eating straight away, makes for a highly memorable meal.*

Smoking can be done in a small portable Box Smoker with a minimum mess. I have an excellent small gas smoker-cum-barbecue, although it's quite easy to adapt an old large square biscuit tin or foil-lined wok.

Seasonings and other flavours are best added to the trout before smoking. A mixture of spices and herbs can be sprinkled over the cleaned fish, or it can be marinated in a blend of oil, lemon juice and herbs and spices. The kind of wood you use for the smoke will subtly affect the flavour. A very popular wood in New Zealand is manuka — either in the form of dry sawdust or chips. It's fun to experiment, but of course the golden rule is to use natural, untreated timber or sawdust.

Place a layer of chips or sawdust in the bottom of the smoker. Position a rack in the middle for the trout to lie on, and fit the lid over. Heat is applied underneath. When the smoking process has started, most trout take 10–20 minutes to be cooked, but check the trout during smoking for doneness, as it can dry out quickly and taste very acrid if overdone.

Trout, straight from the smoker to the plate, with just a squeeze of lemon or one of the following sauces, is one of the best meals imaginable.

The crunchy and slightly earthy flavour of **TROUT WITH PINE NUTS** is evocative of New Zealand's great outdoors.

# TROUT WITH PINE NUTS

4 trout fillets
flour for dredging fillets
salt and ground white pepper
100 g butter
¼ cup oil
50 g butter
½ cup pine nuts
2 tablespoons white wine
1 tablespoon finely chopped chives
1 tablespoon finely chopped parsley
2 teaspoons fresh lemon juice

Dredge the fillets in flour and salt and pepper, shaking off excess. In a large frypan heat 100 g butter and oil over a medium heat until it is sizzling and hot, but not smoking. Sauté fillets skin-side up to 2 minutes. Turn and cook other side for a further 2 minutes or more, until the trout flesh just starts to flake. Transfer to four heated plates.

To the frypan add the extra 50 g butter and nuts. Cook over a medium heat until the nuts begin to brown. Remove them from the pan, stir in the wine, chives, parsley and lemon juice. Spoon this sauce over the fillets and garnish with the pine nuts.

***Serves 4***

## SIMPLE TROUT FILLETS WITH OATMEAL COATING

Skin trout fillets, dip in milk then coarse oatmeal and panfry in a mixture of butter and oil.

Another very simple method of cooking trout is to stuff it and bake it whole. I use all sorts of concoctions for the stuffing: lots of citrus — lemon and limes, grapefruit and orange — mushrooms, breadcrumbs, herbs, capsicum, olives, etc. Wrap fish in oiled foil and bake in oven for approximately 30–35 minutes, depending on size of fish.

## FRESHLY CAUGHT BARBECUE-GRILLED TROUT

After gutting trout and removing the head, carefully clean the body cavity and open the fish out by cutting down the backbone. Lay the fish on the grill, skin-side down, sprinkle the surface with salt and freshly ground black pepper, some fresh chopped herbs — tarragon is particularly nice — and a squeeze of fresh lemon or lime juice. Dot with butter and grill for 10–14 minutes until cooked.

This is a very simple but delicious preparation of fresh trout and it can be easily adapted to oven grilling. A little chopped bacon on the surface adds an interesting flavour to the trout.

## TROUT COOKED IN ASHES

Wrap trout in foil, then in several thicknesses of wet newspaper, or large fresh green leaves or sweetcorn husks (silk and cobs removed). Bury in hot ashes for 20 minutes. Unwrap (most of the skin will come off with the foil) and lift on to serving plates. Trout cooked in this way is deliciously juicy, with a slightly smoky taste.

# S A U C E S  F O R  S M O K E D  T R O U T

## C A P E R  S A U C E

2 egg yolks
1 tablespoon white wine vinegar
½ teaspoon dry mustard
3 tablespoons horseradish sauce
salt and finely ground white pepper
¾ cup light olive oil
1–2 tablespoons capers
2 tablespoons chopped fresh parsley

Place egg yolks, vinegar, mustard, horseradish sauce and salt and pepper in a blender or food processor. Mix until well combined. With the motor running, gradually add oil in a thin, slow stream. Add the capers and parsley and process until capers are finely chopped.

**Makes about 1 cup**

## L E M O N  T H Y M E  M A Y O N N A I S E

1 cup prepared mayonnaise
3 tablespoons natural yoghurt
juice and grated zest of 2 large lemons
salt and freshly ground black pepper to taste
1 tablespoon finely chopped lemon thyme,
    or 1 teaspoon dried thyme with a pinch
    of lemon-pepper seasoning

Mix all ingredients together in a blender or food processor and chill to allow flavours to develop.

**Makes about 1 cup**

## O R A N G E  H O L L A N D A I S E

2 egg yolks
grated zest and juice of 1 large juicy orange
1 teaspoon white wine vinegar
salt and freshly ground black pepper to taste
300 g melted butter
1 tablespoon chopped parsley

Thoroughly mix yolks, zest, juice, vinegar and salt and pepper in a blender or food processor. With the motor running, gradually add the melted butter in a steady stream. Add chopped parsley and taste to check seasoning. A dash of orange-flavoured liqueur such as Cointreau is a luxury addition for a splendid smoked trout dinner.

**Makes about 1 cup**

# D E S S E R T S

Desserts are my passion. Food is so much more than just fuel and a scrumptious dessert, of all things, really makes people sit up and take notice. Over the last two years or so a number of dessert restaurants have sprung up throughout the country and their growing popularity further proves my point that most of us love to indulge our craving for sweet things.

We are lucky enough to have a fabulous range of fresh fruit available in this country all-year round. When the occasion demands dessert, it's hard to beat a pile of glistening fresh fruit, arrayed invitingly on a platter to make the most of the different colours and textures. But while fruits, sorbets and similar light desserts often meet the need for a sweet afterthought, sometimes you just have to recapture the comfort of a sweet cake or a hot, bubbling spicy apple pie — and isn't Mum's home-made apple pie the ultimate cure-all for world weariness?

Then, in a category all by itself, there's chocolate. There has to be more in it than just caffeine to make us react the way we do when the magic word is uttered. Few other foods can evoke the sort of response that chocolate inspires — it's the choice of millions. Who can resist the offer of a dessert that goes by the name of Chocolate Decadence? It seems to be a substance that lends itself to over-the-top descriptions such as "heavenly, scrumptious, delectable, irresistible, luscious, divine" and, of course, let's not forget the afore-mentioned "decadent".

Whatever the occasion, the scope for making a truly irresistible dessert is only limited by your imagination.

# FAY'S SPICED APPLE SHORTCAKE

*This is my mother Fay's recipe. It's our family's absolute favourite pud, and the one most requested for birthdays and special family meals.*

*Canned apple pie filling may be used as a short cut. Other fruit can be substituted for the apple, such as rhubarb, gooseberries, peaches, nectarines, etc. Just sweeten your choice of fruit to personal taste.*

*As the pastry is roughly rolled out and patchworked, this shortcake has a very nice farmhouse kind of feel to it. If you're fortunate enough to have any leftovers, this is a fabulous breakfast treat.*

## SHORTCAKE PASTRY

*125 g butter*
*125 g sugar*
*1 egg*
*1½ cups flour*
*2 tablespoons cornflour*
*1 tablespoon custard powder*
*1 teaspoon baking powder*

## FILLING

*800 g (approximately 4 cups) lightly stewed apple, well drained*
*1 teaspoon mixed spice*
*¼ teaspoon ground cloves*
*icing sugar to decorate*

Preheat oven to 200°C. Beat butter and sugar until creamy. Add the egg, then the sifted dry ingredients. Mix until the soft pastry forms into a ball. Roughly roll out and pat two-thirds of the pastry to line the base and up the sides of a 23–25 cm quiche or pie plate.

To make the filling, in a large saucepan bring the stewed apple gently to the boil, stir in spices and while bubbly and hot, pour over shortcake mixture in pie plate.

Roughly roll out the remaining third of the pastry and place over the hot filling, patchworking small pieces to fill in any gaps. Bake 20–25 minutes until pastry is golden brown. Cool in the pie plate and sprinkle with icing sugar to serve. Whipped cream or ice-cream is the ideal accompaniment and sprinkling a little mixed spice over the cream is a nice touch.

**Serves 6–8**

# INDIVIDUAL STEAMED FRUIT PUDDINGS

6 tablespoons jam, conserve, marmalade or
    jelly
few teaspoons water or liqueur of your choice
fruit of your choice
125 g butter, chilled
1 cup self-raising flour
1 cup fresh white breadcrumbs
½ cup brown sugar
1 egg
2 tablespoons milk
lightly whipped cream to garnish

Well-grease six small individual ramekins or moulds. Soften the jam in a small saucepan or in the microwave. Add a few teaspoons water or liqueur and mix well. Add fruit and allow to cool. Spoon equally into ramekins.

To make the dough, rub butter into flour, add breadcrumbs and sugar. Beat egg and milk together and mix into dry ingredients (this can all be done very easily in a food processor).

Spoon dough evenly over fruit mixture in each ramekin. Place ramekins in a roasting pan and carefully fill it with hot water to come three-quarters of the way up the sides of the ramekins. Cover the whole roasting pan with tinfoil and bake at 180°C for 45 minutes.

To serve, remove puddings from oven and allow to stand for 5 minutes. Carefully tip out on to serving plates and garnish with softly whipped cream.

**Serves 6**

# STICKY DATE PUDDING

180 g dates, stoned and roughly chopped
1 teaspoon baking soda
150 ml boiling water
125 g butter
125 g sugar
2 eggs
125 g self-raising flour

SAUCE

300 g brown sugar
50 g butter
1 cup cream
1 teaspoon vanilla essence

In a bowl sprinkle the dates with the soda, then pour the boiling water over them. Stir until soda is all dissolved and allow to stand for 15–20 minutes. Beat butter and sugar until creamy. Add eggs one at a time, beating until light and fluffy. Stir in the flour, then the soaked dates and water mixture.

Pour into a deep, well-greased and floured 20 cm cake tin. Bake at 190°C for 30–35 minutes or until a skewer inserted into the centre of pudding comes out clean. Allow pudding to stand in tin while you prepare the sauce.

To make sauce, combine all ingredients in a saucepan and stir over a medium heat until sugar is dissolved. Bring to the boil. Turn down and simmer for 5 minutes. Pour a little of the sauce over cooked pudding, then put it back in oven for a few minutes to allow sauce to soak in and bubble to a golden-brown colour. To serve cut the pudding into squares or wedges, depending on shape of the tin. Serve with the extra sauce and lightly whipped cream.

**Serves 4–6**

# PEACH COBBLER

*A really easy country-kitchen-type dessert, made in a jiffy with that old 'just like Mum used to make' quality and you can use almost any other fruit if desired.*

6 large peaches, peeled and sliced
½ cup brown sugar
1 cup flour
¾ cup castor sugar
2 teaspoons baking powder
½ teaspoon salt
1 egg, lightly beaten
100 g butter
¼ cup milk
icing sugar to decorate

Arrange peach slices in a buttered pie dish and sprinkle with the brown sugar. Bake at 180°C for 20 minutes.

While peaches are baking, combine flour, castor sugar, baking powder, salt, egg, butter and milk into a loose dough mixture. This can easily be done in a food processor.

Remove peaches from oven and spoon dough mixture roughly over the top of them. Return to the oven for a further 25 minutes until golden brown and crisp. Sprinkle with icing sugar while hot. Serve with whipped cream or ice-cream.

**Serves 4–6**

**PEACH COBBLER,** *pictured left, is a heavenly way to serve peaches if you love their flavour as much as I do. Garnish portions with* **FRESH PEACH ICE-CREAM** *(page 109) and slices of fresh fruit and it's a real farmhouse dessert.*

**FIGS IN PORT** *look elegant served any time of year.*

# FIGS IN PORT

*A simple, aromatic dessert when figs are fresh and plentiful. I preserve figs in a sugar syrup with alcohol — port, brandy or liqueur are good. These figs are great to open out of season for a dead-easy dessert. All you need is a pretty serving dish and a bowl of whipped cream or sweetened natural yoghurt.*

12 fresh figs
½ cup brown sugar
½ teaspoon cinnamon
200 ml port

Wash figs and with a sharp knife cut a cross in the flesh of each fig at the stalk end (as you do with brussels sprouts) and arrange in a single layer in an ovenproof casserole-type dish. Sprinkle with brown sugar and cinnamon and pour the port over. Cover the dish and bake in the oven at 180°C for approximately 30 minutes. The figs open up like flowers and the port, cinnamon and sugar form a delicious syrup. Serve warm with a little of the syrup ladled over.

Use quantities as a guideline only and replace brown sugar with plain sugar if using a lighter liqueur flavouring, for example Grand Marnier. Adjust the sugar and alcohol amounts to personal taste.

If preserving figs, make the cut in the stalk end, then poach for 20–25 minutes in the liquid. Spoon figs into sterilised jars and use the overflow method to seal them.

**Serves 4–6**

# LEMON CHESS PIE

*This pie can be served either warm with ice-cream or it makes a delicious cold dessert cut in an elegant wedge and garnished with a lemon leaf or tiny sprig of lemon blossom if in season. Lemon sorbet or gelato is particularly good with it.*

PASTRY

125 g butter
1 cup flour
½ cup icing sugar

FILLING

juice and zest of 4 large juicy lemons
   (approximately 150 ml)
2 cups castor sugar
2 tablespoons flour
4 eggs
icing sugar to decorate

To make the pastry, whiz butter, flour and icing sugar in a food processor until it clings together in a ball. Press into a greased pie dish or sponge roll tin and bake in a moderate oven, 180°C, for 10–15 minutes until dryish looking and just starting to colour.

To make the filling, mix lemon zest and juice, castor sugar, flour and eggs together and pour into the hot, partially cooked pastry crust. Return to oven for 25–30 minutes until filling has set.

Sprinkle with icing sugar as soon as you remove the pie from the oven and re-sprinkle prior to serving.

**Serves 4–6**

# LEMON ROULADE

butter and flour for baking tin
6 eggs, separated
½ cup castor sugar
grated zest of 1 lemon
2 teaspoons lemon juice
castor sugar for rolling
300 ml cream, whipped
icing sugar for decorating
extra whipped cream and lemon slices to
   garnish

Preheat oven to 150°C. Line a 20×20 cm sponge roll tin with baking paper, butter well and dust with flour. Beat egg yolks with sugar until pale and creamy. Beat egg whites until they hold stiff peaks. Fold together with lemon zest and juice. Spoon mixture into prepared tin and bake for 15–20 minutes. Turn out on to a tea towel sprinkled with castor sugar and gently remove paper. When cold, spread with whipped cream and roll up. Dust with icing sugar before serving.

Serve with extra whipped cream and slices of lemon or lemon leaves and blossoms, if in season, to garnish.

**Serves 4–6**

# PASSIONFRUIT LEMON MERINGUE PIE

PASTRY

2 tablespoons sugar
1 egg
125 g butter, softened
225 g flour
pinch salt
1 teaspoon baking powder

FILLING

400 g can sweetened condensed milk
½ cup fresh lemon juice
1 tablespoon grated lemon zest
½ cup passionfuit pulp
5 egg yolks

MERINGUE

5 egg whites
1½ cups castor sugar

Beat sugar and egg until pale and frothy, in a food processor. Mix butter, flour, salt and baking powder. Add to egg and sugar and process until mixture clumps together in a ball around the blade. Chill for 30 minutes, then press into the base and up the sides of an approximately 23 cm loose-bottomed quiche or cake tin. Chill again for 30 minutes then bake blind for 20–25 minutes in a medium oven, 180°C, until golden and crisp.

Mix all filling ingredients and pour into the cooked pastry shell.

For meringue topping, beat whites until stiff peaks form. Gradually beat in castor sugar until it is all incorporated and mixture is glossy. Pipe over the passionfruit and lemon filling. Bake in a low oven, 130–150°C, for 15–20 minutes until meringue is firm and crisp. Cool in the tin.

Remove when fully cold and serve with whipped cream or ice-cream. Cut with a wet knife and wipe the knife between each cut to neaten the slices through the meringue topping.

**Serves 6–8**

# PUDDYCAKE OLD-FASHIONED STEAMED PUDDING

50 g butter
½ cup sugar
1 egg
½ cup milk
1 cup flour
1 teaspoon baking powder
extra butter
flavouring — 1 cup preserves, jam or stewed
   fruit, or a 400 g can condensed milk

Beat butter and sugar till creamy, add egg and milk, then mix in flour and baking powder. Grease a steamed pudding bowl generously with butter. Spoon in the flavouring of your choice and spoon the batter over this. Seal with the steamed pudding lid or several layers of grease-proof paper tied with string and covered with tinfoil. Steam for 1½ hours. Carefully invert the pudding on to a plate and serve hot with custard, cream or ice-cream.

**Serves 4–6**

## PAVLOVAS

*We couldn't do a New Zealand cookbook without a pavlova recipe. This is a New Zealand, true-blue recipe — developed by us Kiwis. Australians often take the credit for inventing the pavlova — we know different.*

## JO'S PAVLOVA

*A large pavlova with crusty outsides and a chewy centre.*

6 egg whites, at room temperature
¼ teaspoon salt
¼ teaspoon cream of tartar
2 cups castor sugar
1 tablespoon cornflour
1 tablespoon malt vinegar
2 teaspoons vanilla essence
whipped cream

In a large metal, porcelain or glass bowl, whisk egg whites, salt and cream of tartar until soft peaks form. Gradually, a teaspoon at a time, add castor sugar, whisking continuously until all the sugar has been added and incorporated into egg white. The mixture should be very thick, shiny and glossy. Sift cornflour over egg white and fold in, then fold in vinegar and vanilla. Spoon the mixture on to a tinfoil- or baking-paper-covered baking tray, smoothing out to a dinner-plate-sized circle.

Bake in a low oven, 140°C, turning down if the pavlova starts to colour. Bake for 1½ hours, or until crisp and dry, with a cracked top. Cool on the tray, then carefully peel off the paper or tinfoil when cold.

Spread the top generously with whipped cream and garnish as you wish.

### Suggested Toppings:

- Fresh sliced kiwifruit, bananas and passionfruit pulp
- Strawberries, raspberries and blueberries, dusted with icing sugar
- A thin layer of lemon curd spread under the whipped cream and with slices of orange or crystallised citrus peel and mint leaves arranged on top
- Chopped chocolate walnuts and crystallised ginger
- Pink and white marshmallows and fresh raspberries with sugared violets or rose petals
- Slices of feijoas, tamarillos, kiwanos and persimmon would look fabulous for a wintry pavlova

*In our household* **PAVLOVA WITH STRAWBERRIES** *is requested more than any other dessert. It's a hard one to beat.*

### Serves 8–10

*We all know that moderation is supposed to be the name of the game but* **CHOCOLATE TRUFFLE LOAF WITH RASPBERRY SAUCE** *has to be the exception to this rule.*

# CHOCOLATE TRUFFLE LOAF WITH RASPBERRY SAUCE

2 cups cream
3 egg yolks
500 g dark chocolate
½ cup corn syrup, light or dark
125 g butter
¼ cup icing sugar
1 teaspoon vanilla essence

Line an approximately 23×12 cm loaf tin with cling film. Mix ½ cup of the cream with egg yolks. In a small saucepan over a medium heat, stir the chocolate, corn syrup and butter until smooth and well combined. Add egg mixture and stir constantly for a further 3 minutes. Cool to room temperature. Beat remaining cream with icing sugar and vanilla until soft peaks form. Fold into chocolate.

Pour into plastic-lined loaf tin. Refrigerate overnight or chill for 3–4 hours in the freezer. Carefully lift out loaf and peel off cling film. Slice with a hot knife, wipe knife between each slice. Serve with Raspberry Sauce.

Note: Chocolate Truffle Loaf can be flavoured with a little liqueur or essence and served with an appropriately flavoured sauce. Some suggestions are:

- Chocolate Truffle Loaf with peppermint chocolate sauce
- Mocha Loaf with coffee liqueur sauce
- Grand Marnier or Cointreau-flavoured loaf with chocolate sauce, garnished with orange or mandarin segments

## RASPBERRY SAUCE

2 cups fresh or thawed frozen raspberries
¼ cup sugar, or to taste
a few perfect whole raspberries to garnish

In a food processor or blender, purée raspberries with sugar. Strain and chill. Garnish with whole berries.

**Serves 4–6**

### ICE-CREAM

*I adore ice-cream and it's always been more than just another dessert for me. Many of us have memories of the first food we were allowed to eat after we'd had our tonsils out and the favoured food of children's birthday parties with all that bizarre-coloured wobbly jelly. Growing up in Hawke's Bay, we were spoilt with Rush Munro's ice-cream parlour in Hastings. Sunday drives always ended up there and I can still taste the creamy malted-milk flavour or crushed strawberry.*

*One of my treasured and most used kitchen gadgets is an ice-cream machine and I would really recommend one if you're an ice-cream fanatic like me. One of my party tricks for summer entertaining is to have the guests pick their own strawberries or peaches in the garden, then we make the ice-cream to order, while everyone watches. In one of these new electric freezing churns, it's a simple, 30-minute procedure. The constant stirring of the mixture to break up ice crystals is the secret to successful, smooth frozen desserts.*

# BASIC ICE-CREAM BASE

*This recipe is for the sweet cream base that I always use for ice-cream. The fruits and flavours you can add and invent to your heart's content.*

*3 large egg yolks*
*1 cup castor sugar*
*600 ml cream*
*150 ml milk*

Whisk egg yolks and sugar until pale and fluffy, about 3 minutes. Either microwave mixture for 1 minute on High then whisk again, or whisk over a bowl of hot water for a few minutes to dissolve the sugar. Stir in the cream and milk and blend well. Either transfer mixture to an ice-cream machine and freeze, following the manufacturers' instructions, or turn into a freezer-proof container such as a loaf tin or commercial ice-cream tub. Cover and freeze for one hour. Stir mixture well to break up the ice crystals then re-freeze until firm.

**Makes a litre of ice-cream when frozen**

# BANANA AND HONEY ICE-CREAM

*1 portion Basic Ice-cream Base*
*3 over-ripe bananas*
*juice of 1 lemon*
*2 tablespoons liquid honey*

Mash soft bananas, lemon juice and honey together and blend well into the ice-cream base. Freeze as in Basic Ice-cream Base.

# STRAWBERRY CRUSH ICE-CREAM

*2-3 cups mashed strawberries*
*⅓ cup extra castor sugar*
*juice of 1 lemon*
*1 portion Basic Ice-cream Base*

Combine strawberries, sugar and lemon juice in a bowl, cover and refrigerate for 1 hour. Purée strawberries in a blender or thoroughly mash. Stir into the base mixture and freeze as in Basic Ice-cream Base. Don't freeze the strawberries whole as they freeze as solid as bullets.

# ORANGES AND LEMONS ICE-CREAM

*1 portion Basic Ice-cream Base*
*½ cup lemon juice*
*½ cup orange juice*
*1 tablespoon grated lemon zest*
*1 tablespoon grated orange zest*
*2 teaspoons liquid honey*

Blend all ingredients together and freeze as in Basic Ice-cream Base.

# PERSIMMON CINNAMON ICE-CREAM

*1 portion Basic Ice-cream Base*
*1 cup peeled and lightly poached persimmon*
*½ teaspoon cinnamon*

Combine all ingredients and freeze as in Basic Ice-cream Base.

## SORBETS

*Here are some of my favourite recipes showing the versatility of sorbets — as first courses, in between courses and light finishes to summery meals.*

*As with ice-cream, I use a simple sugar base recipe, then add flavours and fruits to taste.*

*Experiment with your own inventions — citrus and herbs, gin and tonic with lemon or lime, tomato and basil, tropical pawpaw and pineapple, etc.*

**FRESH FRUIT SORBETS** *pictured above and opposite, are a light and refreshing alternative to cream and ice-cream accompaniments. They capture the flavour of the fruit in a way that's easy on the palate, especially after a rich meal.*

# BASIC SORBET BASE

*1 cup sugar*
*2 cups water*
*juice of 2 large lemons*
*whites of 2 large eggs, stiffly beaten*

Dissolve sugar in water and allow to cool. Preferably make the night before and keep in the fridge overnight to really chill down.

Mix syrup with lemon juice. Add flavouring at this point. Freeze in ice trays or freezer-proof container until barely solid then stir mixture well to break up ice crystals. Beat egg whites until stiff. Stir into icy sorbet until smooth. Refreeze.

Refreeze sorbet, covered, until ready to serve, or if you have an ice-cream machine transfer syrup and flavouring to bowl of machine and freeze following the manufacturer's instructions until smooth and firm-textured. Then fold in the stiffly beaten egg white until well blended. Serve either immediately from the machine or cover and place in freezer until ready to use. The sorbet may benefit from 5–10 minutes' softening prior to serving if it is very hard.

**Makes about 4 cups**

# KIWIFRUIT SORBET

*6 large, ripe, peeled and chopped kiwifruit*
*1 portion Basic Sorbet syrup*
*juice of 2 large lemons*
*whites of 2 large eggs*

Purée kiwifruit with syrup mixture and lemon juice. Freeze as in Basic Sorbet Base, stirring in the egg white as directed at the end of the freezing process.

## LEMON PASSIONFRUIT SORBET

*1 portion Basic Sorbet syrup (extra syrup may
   be added to taste depending on how tart
   you want the sorbet)*
*grated zest and juice of 6 large lemons*
*pulp from 6–8 ripe passionfruit*
*whites of 2 large eggs*

Mix syrup, lemon zest and juice thoroughly. Freeze as in Basic Sorbet Base, stirring in the egg white as directed at the end of the freezing process.

## RASPBERRY SORBET

*1 punnet ripe raspberries*
*1 portion Basic Sorbet syrup*
*juice of 2 large lemons*
*whites of 2 large eggs*

Purée raspberries with syrup mixture and lemon juice. Freeze as in Basic Sorbet Base, stirring in the egg white as directed at the end of the freezing process.

## STEINLAGER SORBET

*1 can Steinlager*
*1 portion Basic Sorbet syrup*
*juice of 2 large lemons*
*whites of 2 large eggs*

Mix beer, syrup mixture and lemon juice (add more to taste). Freeze as in Basic Sorbet Base, stirring in the egg white as directed at the end of the freezing process.

## WATERMELON AND STRAWBERRY SORBET

*1 punnet well-ripened strawberries*
*400 g skinned and deseeded watermelon*
*1 portion Basic Sorbet syrup*
*juice of 2 large lemons*
*whites of 2 large eggs*

Purée hulled and washed strawberries and watermelon with syrup mixture and lemon juice. Freeze as in Basic Sorbet Base, stirring in the egg white as directed at the end of the freezing process.

# CAPPUCCINO CREAM CHEESE MOUSSE

250 g cream cheese
3 medium-sized egg yolks
½ cup castor sugar
300 ml cream, thickly whipped and well
    chilled
2 tablespoons coffee and chicory essence
whipped cream and grated chocolate or
    chopped nuts to garnish

Have the cream cheese at room temperature or soften in the microwave. Beat the cream cheese, egg yolks and castor sugar together, then add the coffee essence. Fold in whipped cream and pour into wine glasses and serve with a dollop of whipped cream sprinkled with grated chocolate or chopped nuts to garnish.

If you don't have any coffee and chicory essence, you can substitute a coffee liqueur, e.g. Kahlua, or really strong cold espresso-type coffee.

**Makes 6 small portions**

# PERSIMMON MOUSSE

1 ripe persimmon, puréed (approximately
    ½ cup)
150 ml sweetened natural yoghurt
1 tablespoon icing sugar
juice of 1 orange
1 tablespoon gelatine dissolved in the juice
150 ml cream, stiffly whipped
persimmon and extra whipped cream to
    garnish

Mix all ingredients except cream. Chill mixture until almost set, then fold in whipped cream. Spoon into ramekins or glasses and garnish with persimmon and extra whipped cream.

**Makes 6 small portions**

# THE ULTIMATE CHOCOLATE MOUSSE

3 eggs, separated
200 g dark chocolate, melted
100 ml cream, lightly whipped

Stir egg yolks into melted chocolate until well blended. Whisk egg whites until stiff, fold into chocolate mixture until evenly blended. Fold in whipped cream and spoon into small bowls or glasses to set.

This is very rich so a little goes a long way. For special presentation, serve in liqueur glasses or tiny demi-tasse coffee cups.

**Serves 6 small portions**

# NIBBLES TO HAVE WITH DRINKS

A drinks party is a great way to entertain, day or night, and I'm delighted to see that the cocktail party is currently enjoying a revival. I've also noticed that many special occasions such as weddings, christenings and birthdays are now celebrated in this way.

The New Zealand-style drinks party tends to be a laid-back, relaxed affair. However, it's important to give your guests something to eat when you're serving alcohol. You can use any artistic talent you might have to create beautiful-looking nibbles — my own particular interest lies in achieving a distinctive geometric presentation. I get incredible personal satisfaction from the symmetry of rows of attractive-looking nibbles presented on my ever-growing collection of trays and platters. But there are also plenty of occasions where I'm more casual about it, and that's fine, too.

People are inclined to be more adventurous in trying new food when it's just a one-bite morsel. It seems to me an ideal opportunity to re-create the exotic in a home-base context so that those who might baulk at a Japanese dinner will be much more inclined to try just a bite of sushi for the first time. New tastes and textures can often be happy surprises! The bar and restaurant scene have paved the way for this with the "taste and sip" concept proving to be very popular. Tapas and mezzes are good examples of this.

Your choice of pre-dinner snacks is also very important because first appearances are everything. After you've given your guests tasty tidbits of caviar and/or smoked salmon to nibble on, you can then get away with following up with beans on toast!

## INTERESTING DIPS OR SPREADS

*The following recipes are ideal for filling pastry tart shells or bread cases, small choux pastry puffs or store-bought pastry cases and vol-au-vents. They can be spread on toasted pita bread, crackers, rice crackers, rye bread or home-made water or cheese biscuits.*

## BLUE CHEESE AND DRAMBUIE DIP

*250 g blue vein cheese*
*250 g cream cheese*
*¼ cup Drambuie (or to taste)*

Blend blue vein cheese and cream cheese together in a blender or food processor with Drambuie to taste. The combination of tastes is quite special but do experiment with other liqueurs.

## AVOCADO CREAM CHEESE DIP

*3–4 ripe avocados*
*250 g cream cheese*
*juice and grated zest of 2 small lemons*
*salt and freshly ground black pepper to taste*

Process the avocado, cream cheese, lemon juice and zest in a blender or food processor until smooth and creamy. Season to taste.

## SMOKED FISH CREAM CHEESE SPREAD

*250 g cream cheese*
*2 cups flaked smoked fish fillets (discard any bones)*
*1 tablespoon finely chopped parsley*
*juice and grated zest of 2 small lemons*
*freshly ground black pepper to taste*

Mix all ingredients in a blender or food processor until smooth and creamy. Check seasoning and adjust as necessary.

# COTTAGE CHEESE AND FRESH HERB SPREAD

250 g cottage cheese
½ cup chopped fresh herbs such as parsley,
    chervil, basil, mint, chives, thyme, etc.
salt and pepper to taste

Purée cottage cheese and fresh herbs together in a blender or food processor until smooth and creamy and no curds remain in the cheese. If the mixture is too crumbly and dry, a little milk may be added to help produce the smoothness required. Season with salt and pepper.

# SMOKED EEL PÂTÉ

250 g smoked eel plus a few pieces to garnish
50 g butter
2 spring onions, finely sliced
few drops Tabasco
freshly ground black pepper
2 tablespoons whisky
4 tablespoons cream
2 teaspoons lemon juice
fresh dill to garnish

Remove skin and bones from eel. Melt butter in a frypan, add spring onions and fry for 1 minute. Add smoked eel and fry gently for 2 minutes. Stir in Tabasco and black pepper. Add whisky to the pan and ignite; when flames subside, stir in cream and lemon juice. Remove from heat and cool slightly. Purée mixture in a blender or food processor and spoon into a pâté dish. Refrigerate until firm. Remove from refrigerator about 30 minutes before serving to allow the pâté to soften slightly. Garnish with sprigs of fresh dill. Serve with crusty bread or crackers.

**Serves 8–10**

# SMOKED SALMON PÂTÉ

*This makes good use of any smoked salmon offcuts. Weigh the bits and use an equal amount of butter or softened cream cheese. Any smoked fish such as hapuka roe or smoked marlin can be made into pâtés or spreads like this.*

equal quantities of:
    smoked salmon off-cuts
    butter or softened cream cheese
freshly milled black pepper
2–3 good dashes Tabasco
2 teaspoons lemon juice

In a food processor, make a fine purée of the fish and butter or cream cheese. Season with pepper, Tabasco and lemon juice. Press into a pot. Cover with cling film and refrigerate until ready for use. Serve at room temperature with fingers of hot brown buttered (or dry) toast, or use as a cocktail sandwich filling or for canapés.

# COCKTAIL MUFFINS

*Using the basic toasted cheese muffin recipe, these darling little muffins are also an ideal vehicle for a lovely plump, fat Bluff oyster on a little pillow of sour cream.*

*2 cups flour*
*4 teaspoons baking powder*
*½ teaspoon salt*
*1 egg*
*¼ cup oil*
*1¼ cups milk*
*1 cup grated tasty cheese*
*extra grated cheese to top each muffin*

Mix all ingredients until just blended, but don't overwork the mixture. It should be quite runny and pourable, not too dry. Add a little extra milk to achieve this desirable consistency. Spoon into 36 non-stick mini-muffin tins. Place a few shreds of grated cheese on the top of each muffin and bake at 200°C for 10–15 minutes until puffed and golden brown. Tip out and cool on a wire rack.

### Suggested Fillings:

- Smoked salmon, sour cream and caviar
- Salmon caviar or roe with sour cream
- Softened cream cheese or sour cream with smoked fish, oysters, crabmeat or crayfish
- Cream cheese, sun-dried tomato and fresh basil and pine nuts
- Smoked chicken and marmalade
- A little sliver of wild duck or game with redcurrant jelly.

### Makes 36 mini-muffins

Left: *A drinks party with substantial nibbles is a wonderful way to celebrate an outdoor wedding.*

Opposite: *These attractively presented cocktail nibbles include* COCKTAIL MUFFINS, TINY FILLED BREAD CASES, DRIED APRICOTS WITH CREAM CHEESE *and* BACON AND WATERCHESTNUTS *(page 120).*

# CHEESE BISCUITS FOR DRINKS PARTIES

*My Granny Win Matson gave me this easy recipe from which masses of variations can be produced.*

100 g tasty cheese, grated
100 g chilled butter, grated
100 g flour
pinch of cayenne pepper
salt to taste

Mix first three ingredients thoroughly together, ideally in a food processor, and season to taste with cayenne pepper and salt. Roll into balls, then flatten and bake at 180°C for 10–15 minutes until golden and crisp.

**Variations:**

Add any of the following:
• Crushed potato or corn chips
• Finely diced onion or chives
• Garlic salt
• Lemon pepper or herbs
• Sesame or poppyseeds pressed on top

***Makes about 20***

# DRIED APRICOTS WITH CREAM CHEESE AND PECANS

*250 g cream cheese, softened*
*36 plump, dried apricots*
*36 pecan nut halves*
*fresh herb sprigs to garnish*

Pipe or spread softened cream cheese on to each apricot half. Press on a pecan nut and garnish with a tiny sprig of fresh herb such as parsley, dill or thyme.

**Makes 36**

# BACON AND WATER CHESTNUTS

*8 rashers streaky bacon*
*250 g can water chestnuts*
*garlic salt*

Cut each rasher of bacon into four strips. Wrap water chestnuts in bacon and sprinkle with garlic salt. Thread on skewers, leaving a small gap between each. Bake in a hot oven, 200°C, for about 15 minutes until crispy. Turn once to cook evenly. Serve on fresh new individual long bamboo skewers.

**Makes about 32**

# TINY BREAD CASES

*1 loaf thinly sliced club sandwich bread,*
*   brown or white or a mixture of both*
*oil to brush*

Using a round cookie cutter approximately 5–6 cm wide, cut out two rounds from each slice of bread. Carefully press bread rounds into deep mini-muffin trays and brush with oil. Bake in a 150°C oven for approximately 15–20 minutes until crispy and lightly golden. Cool on a wire rack and store in an airtight container until required.

**Suggested Fillings:**

• Cream cheese with fresh or smoked oysters garnished with a sprig of dill
• Pesto topped with cherry tomatoes
• Prawns and tomato with mayonnaise
• Baby scallops marinated in lime juice with coconut cream
• Smoked salmon and cream cheese topped with caviar

# SHRIMP AND LEMON PEPPER MINI QUICHES

*These are a very popular item for cocktail party food. I use my non-stick mini-muffin baking tins as they make the perfect bite-sized little savoury, but any small baking or patty tin could be used.*

*My children love these little 'pies' and I find them a quick and nourishing teatime treat using simple cheese or vegetable fillings.*

*3 sheets frozen flaky pastry, defrosted*
*1 cup grated cheese*
*1 cup cooked tiny shrimps, well drained*
*approximately 2 teaspoons lemon pepper seasoning*
*2 tablespoons finely chopped parsley*
*1 cup cream*
*3 eggs*
*extra chopped parsley to garnish*

Preheat oven to 200°C. With a cookie cutter press out small circles of flaky pastry to fit into the mini-muffin tins. If not using non-stick tins, grease the tins well and press in the pastry circles.

Sprinkle a few shreds of grated cheese into the base of each case then divide the shrimps, a few into each case, and sprinkle with lemon pepper seasoning and finely chopped parsley. Beat cream and eggs together and pour a little into each case, being careful not to spill over the sides or overfill each case. Top each savoury with a few shreds of grated cheese.

Bake until golden and puffed up with the egg filling set. Ease out of the muffin tins as soon as they're cool enough to handle or leave in to rewarm later if not serving immediately.

A fine sprinkling of chopped parsley added just before serving looks good. Serve these savouries just warmed, not so piping hot that people burn their mouths.

## Variations:

- Bacon or ham finely diced with chives
- Pine nut and basil
- Finely shredded spinach and Feta cheese
- Red onion and herbs
- Blue cheese and walnuts
- Smoked fish and a little horseradish in the cream
- Mussels or any shellfish with a little chopped parsley
- Diced red, green and yellow capsicum and chilli
- Camembert cheese and strawberry
- Tinned smoked oysters
- Pickled walnuts and extra cheese

**Makes about 36**

## SUSHI ROLLS

*These little Japanese delicacies are now very popular as cocktail nibbles. All sorts of goodies can be rolled up in a sushi such as seafood, fresh vegetables, fruit and even cheese.*

*2 cups short grain rice*
*3½ cups water*
*1 teaspoon salt*
*½ cup rice vinegar*
*egg roll (made from 1 egg and 1 tablespoon water)*
*5–6 sheets nori (Japanese dried seaweed)*
*5 spring onions, blanched and trimmed*
*2 carrots, cut into sticks and blanched*
*soy sauce*

Rinse the rice under cold running water until the water runs clear. Place rice, water and salt in a heavy saucepan and bring to the boil. Cover and boil gently for 10 minutes. Cool to room temperature and stir rice vinegar through.

To make the egg roll, thoroughly whisk egg and water until well combined. Pour into a non-stick or lightly greased pan and tilt to spread the mixture. Cook for 2–3 minutes over a gentle heat until the egg is set but not browned. Do not turn over but invert the pan onto a paper towel and allow the egg to cool completely. Trim to a rectangular shape and roll up tightly.

To assemble lay the nori sheets, shiny side down, on a clean tea towel. Cover with a cup of cooked rice, spreading evenly over each sheet, leaving 2 cm free at the top. Pat down well. Lay the blanched vegetables and egg roll down the centre. Roll up the nori sheet tightly, using the tea towel. Moisten the edge with water to seal and wrap in cling film. Repeat process with remaining ingredients. Refrigerate until required.

Slice just before serving and arrange attractively on a tray. Serve with a little dish of soy sauce for dipping.

**Makes about 20**

*People are more inclined to try a new taste sensation when it's presented as a bite-size morsel.*

Left: **BLUE CHEESE AND DRAMBUIE DIP** *(page 116) and* **SMOKED EEL PÂTÉ** *(page 117).*

Opposite: **SMOKED SALMON AND CHIVE PARCELS** *(page 123),* **SUSHI ROLLS** *(page 122) and* **CHERRY TOMATO KEBABS** *(page 125).*

# SMOKED SALMON AND CHIVE PARCELS

*It's best to assemble these parcels one at a time, keeping the mixture in the refrigerator in between making each one, so that it stays firm and chilled and therefore easy to work with. Strips of nori (Japanese dried seaweed) can be substituted for the chives.*

*500 g thinly sliced smoked salmon*
*500 g smoked salmon offcuts*
*250 g cream cheese, softened*
*zest of 1 medium-sized lemon*
*salt and freshly ground black pepper*
*15–20 chives, about 20 cm long.*

In a food processor or blender combine the salmon offcuts, cream cheese, zest and the salt and pepper. Process until smooth and well combined. Chill for 1½–2 hours until firm.

Cut the thinly sliced smoked salmon into strips about 2.5 by 8 cm. Arrange two strips at a time on the bench in a cross shape and place a teaspoonful of the cream cheese mixture in the middle of the cross. Fold the ends over and allow to chill. Repeat this process with the rest of the smoked salmon slices and cream cheese mixture. Before serving, tie each parcel up with a chive bow ensuring the folds are underneath. Running hot water over the chives just before you use them makes them more pliable and easier to work with.

**Makes 12–15**

## CROSTINI WITH OLIVADA SPREAD

*The flavour of this delicious spread improves after 24 hours in the refrigerator where it will keep for at least a week. However, it's best eaten at room temperature.*

*1 cup pitted black olives*
*2 cloves garlic, peeled and crushed*
*1 tablespoon capers, drained*
*¼ cup extra virgin olive oil*
*1 tablespoon chopped parsley*
*1 French bread stick, preferably one day old*
*olive oil for brushing*
*strips of red capsicum to garnish*

Combine the olives, garlic and capers in a food processor and whiz for a few seconds to combine. With the motor running, slowly drizzle the olive oil through the feed tube and process until smooth. Stir in the chopped parsley, cover and refrigerate until required.

When ready to serve, cut the bread stick into thin slices. Brush generously with olive oil and bake in a medium oven, 180°C, until crispy golden and dried. Spread the topping thickly onto the toasted crostini and garnish with strips of capsicum.

**Makes 25–30**

## GARLIC MUSSELS IN THE SHELL

*As well as making delicious cocktail nibbles, a plate of these served with a crisp salad and some crunchy bread makes a speedy and satisfying meal.*

*20 mussels in the shell*
*50 g butter, softened*
*2 cloves garlic, peeled and crushed*
*salt and freshly ground black pepper*
*¼ cup coarse dried breadcrumbs*

Scrub the mussels and remove any hairy beards. Cover with cold water and simmer until they open. Remove with a slotted spoon immediately. Break off the top shell and ease the mussel out of the remaining shell.

Mix the butter, garlic and salt and pepper together. Put each mussel back into its half-shell and place a knob of garlic butter on top of each. Sprinkle with breadcrumbs. Place under a hot grill until the butter sizzles and the crumbs are golden. Serve immediately.

**Makes 20**

# SPINACH AND FETA CHEESE IN PHYLLO CUPS

3 sheets phyllo pastry
50 g butter, melted
½ cup cooked spinach, chopped and well
  drained
50–80 g Feta cheese
freshly ground black pepper
2 eggs
2 tablespoons pine nuts (optional)

Lay out a sheet of phyllo on the bench. Brush with melted butter and cover with another sheet. Brush top of second sheet with butter and cover with the third sheet. Using scissors, carefully cut circle shapes out of the pastry, about the diameter of a wine glass. Gently press the pastry circles into a deep non-stick, well-greased mini-muffin tin. Trim any pastry overhang level with the top of the tin.

In a blender or food processor mix the spinach, Feta cheese, black pepper and eggs until smooth and well combined. Fill the phyllo-lined muffin tin with teaspoonfuls of spinach mixture leaving enough room for it to expand and puff up a little. Place a few pine nuts on top of each and bake in a medium-hot oven, 180–120°C, for 8–10 minutes until the filling is set and the phyllo crispy and golden. Leave in the tin for a minute or so then serve immediately or allow to completely cool and then reheat for later use.

**Makes 12**

# CHERRY TOMATO KEBABS

*These little nibbles have a distinctive Mediterranean flavour which the black olives, if you decide to use them, complement really well.*

100 g Mozzarella cheese
20 small ripe cherry tomatoes
20 small fresh basil leaves
10 black olives, pitted and cut in half
  (optional)

Cut the Mozzarella into 20 small cubes. Thread one of each of the Mozzarella cubes and cherry tomatoes, with a basil leaf in between, onto toothpicks or cocktail sticks. If using olives, these may be placed between the cube of Mozzarella and the basil leaf.

**Makes 20**

# BAKING

*My mother was my first great teacher in the kitchen. I have many happy memories: watching the batter gently cascade in a silken movement from the old Kenwood mixer, adding the vanilla or chocolate chips to the mixture, scraping and licking the bowl, pressing biscuits on a tray with a fork, and generally doing other helpful things while she baked to "fill the tins". It's interesting to note that rubber scrapers (or spatulas) have always been known as "meanies" in our household — my grandmother coined the name because their efficiency meant that there was nothing left for us to lick from the bowl!*

*Everyone appreciates a home-made cake, whether it's for a special morning tea at the office or for dessert. Chances are that your favourite recipe has been handed down in the family or acquired from old friends. There's great personal pleasure in baking and more and more people are discovering the joys in hands-on bread making as well. The smells that waft through the house after a bout of baking are truly evocative of a country kitchen.*

*Most New Zealand children grow up with biscuits forming part of their daily diet. I love making them for my family, packed with oats, raisins, honey and other goodies. They just can't compare with the ones from the supermarket which, among other things, lack that essential buttery taste.*

*Baking was a large part of our everyday lives and continues to be in most country households today: there's morning tea (and "smoko" for the blokes), afternoon tea, and, of course, the two New Zealand traditions of baking to "fill the tins" and when an invitation asks you to "bring a plate" to a local event.*

## CHOCOLATE CHUNK OAT COOKIES

*I'm always getting requests to make batches of these cookies for all the local fundraising fêtes.*

250 g butter
3 tablespoons condensed milk
¾ cup sugar
1½ cups flour
1½ cups rolled oats
1 teaspoon baking powder
250 g dark chocolate, roughly chopped, or
   large-sized chocolate chips

Beat butter, condensed milk and sugar together until light and creamy. Add flour, rolled oats, baking powder and chocolate chunks. Flatten dessertspoonfuls of mixture on to a well greased oven tray and cook for 15–20 minutes in a medium oven, 180°C, until golden brown. Cool on a wire rack and store in an airtight container.

**Makes about 24**

## CHOCOLATE FUDGE BROWNIES

*This makes a fabulous base for a dessert — just add a scoop of ice-cream and Chocolate Fudge Sauce. Garnish with strawberries or raspberries. Brownies can also be iced or frosted.*

200 g dark chocolate
200 g butter
2 cups sugar
3 eggs
1 teaspoon vanilla essence
1 cup flour
1 cup chopped nuts (optional)

Melt chocolate and butter together, stir until smooth and well blended. Mix in sugar, eggs and vanilla, then stir in flour and nuts. Pour into a well-greased, approximately 20×30 cm sponge-roll tin. Bake at 180°C for 20–35 minutes or until a skewer inserted in the centre comes out with fudgy crumbs. Cool in the tin and cut into squares. Store in an airtight container.

**Makes about 15**

# THELMA'S SHORTBREAD

250 g butter, softened
¾ cup icing sugar
½ cup cornflour
1½ cups flour

Beat butter and icing sugar until creamy. Mix in cornflour and flour. On a floured surface roll out dough to 1 cm thick and cut into fingers. Carefully place on a greased oven tray. Prick with a fork. Bake at 150°C for 25–30 minutes, until shortbread is pale but crisp. Cool on a wire rack and store in an airtight container.

**Makes about 20–24**

# ANZAC BISCUITS

*These delicious crunchy biscuits can be dipped in chocolate or topped with fudge icing for a special treat. I've even made double-dipped Anzacs, first coated in milk chocolate, then a second dip in dark chocolate, for an ultra-extravagant Christmas version.*

50 g flour
80 g sugar
⅔ cup coconut
⅔ cup rolled oats
1 teaspoon baking soda
2 tablespoons boiling water
2 tablespoons golden syrup
50 g butter, melted

Mix flour, sugar, coconut and rolled oats together. In another bowl dissolve baking soda in the boiling water. Stir in golden syrup and melted butter. Mix all ingredients together and place in teaspoonfuls on a well-greased or non-stick oven tray. Bake at 180°C for approximately 15 minutes until golden brown. Cool on a wire rack and store in an airtight container.

**Makes about 24.**

# HOKEY POKEY BISCUITS

125 g butter
50 g sugar
1 tablespoon milk
1 tablespoon golden syrup
1 teaspoon baking soda
1½ cups flour

Beat butter and sugar until creamy. Heat milk and golden syrup together and add baking soda. Mix well with creamed butter and sugar, add flour. Roll into small balls on a greased oven tray. Press flat with a wet fork. Bake at 180°C for 12–15 minutes. Cool on a wire rack and store in an airtight container.

**Makes about 24**

## FAY'S MUMBLES

*125 g butter*
*1 cup sugar*
*2 tablespoons golden syrup*
*1 cup flour*
*1 teaspoon baking powder*
*1 cup coconut*
*1 egg*
*1 cup mixed dried fruit, such as raisins,*
  *currants, etc*
*5 Weetbix or equivalent dry wholewheat*
  *breakfast cereal, crushed*

Melt butter, sugar and golden syrup in a large saucepan. Add all other ingredients and mix thoroughly Press into a greased flat sponge-roll-type baking tin, approximately 30×20 cm. Bake at 180°C for 20 minutes. Cut into bars while still warm. Store in an airtight container.

**Makes about 20**

## GINGER GEMS

*1½ cups flour*
*1 teaspoon baking powder*
*1 teaspoon ground ginger*
*1 egg*
*½ cup milk*
*25 g butter, melted*
*2 tablespoons golden syrup*
*25 g brown sugar*

*Ginger gems and scones are always on the menu for morning and afternoon teas for farm workers at shearing or haymaking time.*

Sift dry ingredients. Beat egg and milk together and stir into dry ingredients. Melt butter and golden syrup together, add with sugar to the mixture.

Heat up gem irons. Grease well when hot, then spoon in the mixture. Bake for 12 minutes at 220°C. Tip out and cool on a wire rack. To serve, split and butter.

**Makes about 12**

*My two little helpers, Katie and Guy. Opposite, clockwise:* **ANZAC BISCUITS** *(page 129),* **AFGHAN BISCUITS** *(page 131),* **FAY'S MUMBLES** *(page 130),* **JO'S MINI PECAN PIES** *(page 132) and* **GINGER GEMS** *(page 130).*

# AFGHAN BISCUITS

200 g butter
60 g sugar
1 teaspoon vanilla essence
170 g flour
2 tablespoons cocoa
1 teaspoon baking powder
60 g crushed cornflakes

ICING

1½ cups icing sugar
60 g butter
2 tablespoons boiling water
¼ cup cocoa
walnut halves to decorate

Beat butter and sugar until creamy, add vanilla. Mix in flour, cocoa and baking powder, stir in crushed cornflakes. Place heaped teaspoonfuls of mixture on a greased or non-stick oven tray and bake at 180°C for 12–15 minutes. Cool on a wire rack and store in an airtight container.

To make icing, beat all ingredients together until smooth and spread over cooled biscuits. Top each with a walnut half.

**Makes about 24**

## SPICE BISCUITS

*This is my mother's recipe and our family's biscuit tins are permanently stocked with these bikkies. It makes a good big batch, ideal for Christmas gifts.*

250 g butter
1½ cups sugar
1 egg
1 tablespoon golden syrup
2 cups flour
1 teaspoon baking powder
2 teaspoons mixed spice

Beat butter and sugar until creamy, add egg and golden syrup, then mix in dry ingredients. Roll teaspoonfuls of mixture into little balls and place on greased or non-stick oven trays. Flatten with a wet fork. Bake at 180°C for 12–15 minutes until golden brown. Cool on a wire rack. Store in an airtight container.

**Makes about 24**

## JO'S MINI PECAN PIES

*These make a great alternative to traditional puddings or heavy desserts at Christmas dinner. Garnish them with holly sprigs and you could serve them with a small dollop of traditional Christmas Hard Sauce.*

125 g butter
1 cup flour
½ cup icing sugar
1 cup pecans
60 g butter, melted
1 large egg
1 cup brown sugar
1 teaspoon vanilla essence

HARD SAUCE

150 g butter
1½ cups sifted icing sugar
¼ cup brandy
¼ cup cream

Whiz butter, flour and icing sugar in a food processor until it clings together in a ball. Divide into 24 pieces, and with floured hands, press into the bases and up the sides of well-greased shallow patty tins. Chill for 15 minutes.

Divide pecans into chilled pastry-lined patty tins, two to three halves in each. Mix melted butter, egg, brown sugar and vanilla together and spoon over the nuts. Bake for 15–20 minutes at 150°C until the pastry is golden brown and the filling puffed and crisp. Cool in the pans until you are able to handle the pies, then carefully push them out of the mould and cool further on a wire rack. They are best eaten warm.

To make Hard Sauce, beat butter to soften. Gradually beat in sifted icing sugar. Continue beating until light and fluffy. Stir in brandy and cream. Spoon into a bowl, cover and chill. This is the traditional accompaniment to Christmas pudding.

**Makes 24**

# PRUNELLA CAKE

*This recipe was given to me by one of my mother's 'sewing gals', a group of friends who meet weekly for a good chat and the chance to do some fine hand sewing and needlework together. A fancy ladies' afternoon tea always plays a big part in the proceedings.*

125 g butter
1 cup sugar
2 eggs
150 g sour cream
1 cup stewed, roughly chopped pitted prunes
    (reserve juice)
½ cup flour
½ teaspoon baking soda
½ teaspoon salt
½ teaspoon nutmeg
½ teaspoon cinnamon
½ teaspoon ground allspice

ICING

2 cups icing sugar
25 g butter, softened
½ teaspoon ground cinnamon
reserved strained prune juice, approximately
    3 tablespoons

Preheat oven to 180°C. Beat butter and sugar until creamy. Add eggs, sour cream and prunes. Fold in sifted dry ingredients. Spoon into two well-greased and floured 20-cm sandwich tins.

Bake for 30–35 minutes until firm and cooked through the centre. Test by inserting a skewer which should come out clean. Tip out on to a wire rack to cool.

To make icing, thoroughly beat all ingredients until smooth and spreadable. Use icing to sandwich cakes together and spread another layer on top.

*This* **SOUTHERN COMFORT CAKE**, *instead of being frosted, can be given a spectacular Christmas presentation by piling nuts and glacé fruit on top and drizzling all over with caramelised sugar as pictured here.*

# SOUTHERN COMFORT CAKE

*1 kg mixed dried fruit*
*2 tablespoons mixed peel*
*100 g glacé cherries, red and green if possible*
  *(use more if you like them)*
*1½ cups Southern Comfort or substitute*
  *brandy, rum or liqueur of your choice*
*grated zest and juice of 1 orange*
*2 teaspoons vanilla essence*
*250 g butter*
*250 g brown sugar*
*4 eggs*
*4 mashed bananas*
*375 g flour*
*1 teaspoon mixed spice*
*½ teaspoon baking powder*

## SOUTHERN COMFORT FROSTING

*250 g butter, softened*
*⅓ cup Southern Comfort liqueur*
*3–3½ cups icing sugar*

Soak fruit, peel and cherries overnight in the Southern Comfort, vanilla, orange zest and juice. Beat butter and sugar until creamy, add eggs one at a time, beating well, then mashed bananas and fruit soaked in Southern Comfort. Stir in dry ingredients and mix well.

Pour into a well-greased and paper-lined large round or square Christmas cake tin, approximately 25 cm. Wrap *outside* of tin in four to five sheets of newspaper tied around with string. Bake for 2½–3 hours at 150°C, turning down to 120°C after 30 minutes if the cake is colouring too fast. The cake should be very moist, but it will pull away from the sides of the tin when cooked. Leave to cool in the oven. Turn off.

To make frosting, beat softened butter, Southern Comfort and 3 cups icing sugar together, adding extra icing sugar to get a smooth spreading consistency. Spread lavishly over top and sides of cake, using a palette knife to swirl frosting into decorative peaks.

For a simple wedding cake, I tie soft ribbons around the cake and surround it with fresh flowers and greenery, old-fashioned roses, baby's breath, cornflowers, gypsophila, etc. depending on the mood and colour scheme of the wedding.

Note: Change the flavour of the icing according to whatever alcohol you have used in the cake.

# MRS BUTTON'S BILLY SPONGE

*Originally this would have been cooked in a billy in a camp oven or coal range. We make ours in a standard loaf tin which makes for easy slicing. I often use a slice of Billy Sponge as a base for an easy dessert; just adding some fresh or poached fruit and ice-cream or whipped cream. It's also great toasted and eaten with bacon, bananas and maple syrup for a party brunch or breakfast. I love the cracked sugar coating and rather chewy texture of this really simply made cake.*

4 eggs
1 cup sugar
1 cup flour
½ teaspoon baking powder

Well grease an approximately 12×23 cm loaf tin and sprinkle sides and base with sugar. Beat eggs until pale and fluffy and slowly add the sugar. Fold in sifted flour and baking powder. Pour into the greased and sugared tin. Sprinkle extra sugar over the top of the mixture and bake at 180°C for 35–40 minutes until the top is golden and crunchy and the loaf cooked through. Tip out and cool on a wire rack.

**MRS BUTTON'S BILLY SPONGE** *goes back a long way in my family and is favoured above any other more complicated recipes.*

## EASY APPLE CINNAMON CAKE

125 g butter, melted
2 cups, approximately, well-drained slightly
    stewed apple or canned apple pie filling
1 cup sugar
1 egg
1¼ cups flour
2 teaspoons ground cinnamon
1½ teaspoons baking powder
½ cup sultanas
icing sugar to decorate

Mix all ingredients together and spoon into a well-greased 20–23 cm paper-lined cake tin. Bake at 150°C for 40–45 minutes or until golden and well cooked in the centre. It is done when a skewer inserted in the centre comes out clean. Cool on a wire rack. Serve warm, sprinkled with icing sugar.

## CHOCOLATE DECADENCE FUDGE CAKE

*This is the wonderful dense, ultra-chocolatey cake often used as the basis of desserts. Serve with fudge sauce and whipped cream.*

250 g dark chocolate
185 g butter
¾ cup raw sugar
6 eggs, separated
2 cups finely ground almonds

CHOCOLATE FUDGE
SAUCE

300 ml cream
375 g dark chocolate
whipped cream and shaved or chopped
    chocolate to decorate

Preheat oven to 180°C. Melt chocolate and butter together, and stir until smooth. Stir in raw sugar and egg yolks, then ground almonds. The mixture will be very thick and sticky.

Beat egg whites until stiff. Stir quarter of the egg white into the chocolate mixture to soften it slightly, then carefully fold in remaining egg white. Spoon into a well-greased and paper-lined 23–25 cm loose-bottomed cake tin.

Bake for 1 hour. The cake does not rise very much and appears shrunken and cracked on the top. Don't panic! this is normal. Cool the cake in the tin. Carefully remove from tin and peel off paper when quite cold.

Place cream and chocolate in a saucepan and stir with a wire whisk over very gentle heat, until the chocolate melts and is well combined with the cream.

Cool for 30 minutes then spread over the top and drizzle down the side of the cake, then chill the cake for 2 hours.

Serve the cake in small wedges, bearing in mind this is an extremely rich cake. But just watch them coming back for seconds. Serve with whipped cream and remaining Chocolate Fudge Sauce, and decorate with shaved or coarsely chopped chocolate. The chocolate sauce needs to be warmed to be pourable as it sets solid at room temperature.

# APRICOT RICOTTA CAKE

600 g Ricotta cheese (or well-drained cottage
   cheese)
3 whole eggs
9 eggs, separated
2 cups dried apricots, finely chopped or
   minced
1 cup crystallised peel
zest and juice of 2 oranges
1 cup sugar
1 cup flour
½ cup sliced almonds for topping

Place Ricotta cheese, whole eggs, egg yolks, apricots, peel, orange zest and juice, sugar and flour in a large bowl and mix well. This can be done in a large food processor.

Beat egg whites until stiff, then fold carefully into main mixture. Spoon into a well-greased and floured 23–25 cm loose-bottomed tin. Sprinkle with sliced almonds and bake at 180°C for approximately 45 minutes until the centre feels firm and set. Cool in the tin.

Delicious served with an apricot purée and whipped cream.

# BANANA CAKE WITH LEMON FROSTING

*Ripe, over-the-top bananas give the best flavour. You can keep them in the freezer until you have 3 for the recipe.*

125 g butter
1 cup brown sugar
1 teaspoon vanilla essence
2 eggs
3 ripe bananas, mashed
¼ cup milk
2 cups self-raising flour
¼ teaspoon salt

LEMON FROSTING

2 cups icing sugar, approximately
100 g butter, softened
grated zest and juice of 2 medium-sized
   lemons

Mix butter and sugar until creamy, add the vanilla, eggs, mashed bananas and milk. Mix well, add the flour and salt. Spoon mixture into a well-greased and paper-lined 20–23 cm square, or a large ring tin.

Bake at 180°C for 35–45 minutes until well cooked in the middle. The centre will spring back when touched. The cooking time varies with different-shaped cake tins, the ring tin cooking fastest.

Great as a speedy dessert, but it is equally delicious if you allow it to cool on a wire rack, then spread with lemon icing.

To make frosting, beat all frosting ingredients together until creamy and smooth. Spread over cooled banana cake.

# CHOCOLATE ZUCCHINI CAKE

*Although this sounds unusual, it's really worth a try. It's a very moist chocky cake that has them lining up for seconds. No problem getting children to eat their greens here.*

125 g butter, softened
1¾ cups sugar
½ cup oil
2 eggs
½ cup milk
1 teaspoon vanilla essence
¼ cup cocoa
2½ cups flour
1 teaspoon baking soda
1 teaspoon mixed spice
2 cups well-scrubbed, grated zucchini (patted
    dry on paper towels)
1 cup chocolate chips
¾ cup chopped walnuts

FROSTING

125 g butter, softened
250 g cream cheese, softened
500 g icing sugar
1 teaspoon vanilla essence
¼ cup cocoa

Beat butter and sugar together until creamy, beat in the oil and eggs. Add the milk and vanilla, stir in the sifted cocoa, flour, baking soda and spice. Fold in the grated zucchini, chocolate chips and walnuts. Pour mixture into two well-greased and paper-lined 23 cm round cake tins.

Bake at 180°C for 25–30 minutes, until a skewer when inserted into the middle comes out clean. Cool for 10 minutes in the tins, then carefully turn out and cool completely on a wire rack.

Beat all the icing ingredients together until fluffy, smooth and well combined. Spread a third of the icing between the cakes and use the remainder to coat the top and sides of the cake.

**WHOLE ORANGE CAKE** *(page 140) is a scrumptious dense cake topped with flaked almonds. It is guaranteed to make a great impression at a smart afternoon tea party.*

*A luxury version of a carrot cake, this* **PECAN PASSIONCAKE WITH CREAM CHEESE FROSTING** *is substantial enough to serve as a special dessert.*

# PECAN PASSIONCAKE WITH CREAM CHEESE FROSTING

*2 cups sugar*
*4 eggs*
*1¼ cups oil*
*225 g can crushed pineapple, drained*
*1 cup chopped pecans or walnuts*
*2 cups flour*
*2 teaspoons baking powder*
*1½ teaspoons baking soda*
*2 teaspoons cinnamon*
*1 teaspoon salt*
*2 cups grated carrot*
*½ cup sultanas*

## CREAM CHEESE FROSTING

*250 g cream cheese, softened*
*100 g butter, softened*
*3 cups icing sugar*
*1 teaspoon vanilla or butterscotch essence*
*chopped pecans to decorate*

Beat sugar and eggs until creamy, add oil and mix well. Stir in pineapple and nuts. Stir in all dry ingredients, followed by carrot and sultanas. Pour into a 23 cm deep greased and paper-lined cake tin.

Bake at 180°C for 1 hour approximately until firm and cooked in the centre. Test by inserting a skewer which should come out clean. Allow to rest in tin for 10 minutes then tip out and cool on a wire rack. Frost when completely cool.

To make frosting, beat all ingredients together until fluffy and creamy. Spread over top and down sides of cake and decorate with chopped pecans.

# RHUBARB AND CINNAMON CAKE

*500 g (approximately 4 stalks) rhubarb, all leaves and green tops discarded as they can be very toxic*
*60 g butter, softened*
*3½ cups brown sugar*
*2 eggs*
*1 teaspoon vanilla essence*
*250 ml sour cream*
*2 cups flour*
*1 teaspoon baking soda*
*1 teaspoon salt*
*1 teaspoon cinnamon*

TOPPING

*1 cup brown sugar*
*2 teaspoons cinnamon*

Wipe rhubarb clean and chop into 2-cm pieces. Mix butter and 400 g brown sugar together, then beat in eggs, vanilla and sour cream. Stir in flour, baking soda, salt and teaspoon of cinnamon; fold in the chopped rhubarb. Spoon mixture into a greased 23–25 cm round loose-bottomed tin.

Mix cup of brown sugar and 2 teaspoons cinnamon together and sprinkle through a coarse sieve evenly over the cake mixture. Bake for 1¼ hours at 180°C, cool in the cake tin. Remove side of tin and carefully ease off the base.

# WHOLE ORANGE CAKE

*2 large sweet oranges*
*6 eggs, separated*
*100 g castor sugar*
*100 g ground almonds*
*50 g fine white breadcrumbs*
*1 teaspoon baking powder*
*½ cup flaked almonds*

*Surrounded by fresh orange or bay leaves with some tiny mandarins or sprigs of orange blossom, this cake looks beautiful.*

Preheat oven to 180°C. Scrub oranges and cover with cold water. Bring to the boil and cook for 15–20 minutes until quite tender. Drain and quarter, remove any obvious pips, but leave peel on. Purée quarters in a food processor.

Beat egg yolks with sugar until light and foamy. Stir in puréed orange and ground almonds. Fold in breadcrumbs with baking powder. Whisk egg whites until stiff, then fold into the mixture. Spoon into a 23 cm paper-lined greased and floured cake tin. Sprinkle with flaked almonds.

Bake for 45 minutes until cake is springy in the centre and just starting to shrink from the sides of the tin. Cool in the tin for a few minutes, then transfer to a wire rack.

Softly whipped cream is the most delicious accompaniment with this cake.

# PIKELETS

*My mother passed on to me her special pikelet recipe — a traditional delicious treat for Sunday afternoon tea with home-made preserves and whipped cream. This recipe makes well risen, fat 'proper' pikelets, with no resemblance to some folk's flattened pancake versions.*

1 teaspoon soda
1 cup milk
1 egg
3 tablespoons sugar
2 cups flour
2 teaspoons cream of tartar

Dissolve soda in milk. Beat in egg and sugar, then mix in flour and cream of tartar. Mix to a smooth batter. Allow to rest for 20 minutes then spoon on to a heated non-stick or well-greased heavy frypan or crêpe pan. Cook over a medium heat until bubbles appear and the surface is golden brown. Turn and cook other side. Cool on a wire rack while you cook the rest of the batch.

### Variation:

Savoury pikelets can be made by leaving out the sugar and replacing it with salt and freshly ground black pepper. Chopped herbs, chilli powder, etc. can also be added. Savoury pikelets are a great base for cocktail food — top with smoked salmon, avocado mousse, etc.

**Makes about 24**

# FARMHOUSE SCONES

*An unusual method taught to me by my friend Sue, who is a scone whiz kid, having initially made millions of scones for shearers then being promoted to chief scone maker at our café in Clevedon.*

3 cups self-raising flour
½ teaspoon salt
25 g butter
approximately 1 cup milk

Sift flour and salt into a large bowl. Stir butter and milk over gentle heat, or microwave until the butter melts. Pour into the flour and mix to a soft dough, adding extra milk (cold) if required. Very gently knead (don't over handle) the dough and press flat to 3 cm thick.

Cut out squares or rounds and place on a cold greased oven tray. Brush with milk and bake at 220°C for 10–15 minutes until golden brown. Cool on the tray. Cover with a clean tea towel which keeps scones soft and moist. These keep well. Microwave for a few seconds to revive as fresh as when just baked.

# FLOWERPOT HERB BREADS

3 teaspoons dried yeast
1 teaspoon sugar
2 cups warm water
5 cups flour, approximately
2 teaspoons salt
2 tablespoons lard
1 cup fresh herbs, chopped (basil, thyme,
    sage, oregano, etc.)
milk

Preheat oven to 180°C. Mix yeast and sugar with water. Set aside. Sift flour and salt into a bowl, then rub in the lard using your fingertips. Add chopped herbs. Mix liquid into flour to make a soft, workable dough. Use a little extra flour if required.

Mix well and turn on to a floured surface. Knead the dough until pliable and elastic, about 10 minutes. Oil a large bowl and roll the dough around in it to coat entire surface. Cover with cling film or a damp tea towel. Allow to rise in a warm, draught-free area until doubled in volume, about 1½ hours.

Remove dough from bowl, punch down and knead for 5 minutes or until the texture is smooth and elastic. Cut dough into pieces about 3 cm in diameter. Roll each piece into a ball and place in small, new, well-greased terracotta flower pots. Cover the pots with a damp tea towel and allow to stand until the dough has risen over the tops of the pots. Brush with milk and bake in preheated oven for 15–20 minutes, or until cooked.

### Makes 8–10 small flowerpot loaves

**FLOWERPOT HERB BREADS** *are easy to make and if terracotta pots are not available, you can improvise with any other small ovenproof dishes.*

# COUNTRY ROSEMARY BREAD

*A flat pizza or foccacia-style bread, great to serve with cheese dishes or to extend a simple salad or soup meal with definite style.*

2 tablespoons dried yeast
1 teaspoon liquid honey
1¼ cups lukewarm water
¾ cup lukewarm milk
2 tablespoons olive oil, plus a little extra
1 teaspoon garlic salt
6 cups flour
1 teaspoon dried rosemary leaves
coarsely ground salt (optional)

Stir yeast, honey and warm water together and set aside for 10 minutes until frothy.

Add the milk, oil and salt, then pour into the flour. Mix with your hands until a soft dough forms. You may need to incorporate a little extra flour. Knead the dough on a floured surface for 10–12 minutes. Oil a large bowl and roll the dough around in it to coat entire surface. Cover bowl with cling film or a damp tea towel. Allow to rise in a warm, draught-free area until doubled in size, approximately 1½–2 hours.

Remove dough from bowl, punch down and knead until smooth, about 1 minute. Return to bowl, cover, and allow to rise again for 1 hour. Divide dough in half and pat out into flattened pizza-like cakes on oven tray. Allow to rise for a further 30 minutes.

Gently pat the surface of the dough with your finger tips, leaving indentations. Drizzle with a little extra olive oil, about a tablespoon for each, and sprinkle with rosemary and, if you like, coarsely ground salt.

Bake at 200°C for 15–20 minutes until golden brown and hollow sounding when tapped. Remove from oven and brush with more olive oil. Break into hearty chunks and eat while fresh and warm.

**COUNTRY ROSEMARY BREAD,** *pictured above.*

## WALNUT BREAD

3 egg whites
½ cup castor sugar
1 cup flour
150 g walnut pieces

Beat egg whites until soft peaks form. Gradually add sugar, a tablespoon at a time. Fold in sifted flour, then carefully fold in nuts. Spread evenly into a well-greased and paper-lined loaf tin, approximately 8×22 cm.

Bake at 180°C for 30 minutes, until light golden brown. Cool on a wire rack. Wrap in tinfoil and stand for 4–6 hours or overnight.

Using an electric knife or a very sharp serrated knife, slice the loaf thinly, approximately 45 slices. Bake the slices on an oven tray for 30–40 minutes at 150°C until crisp and dry. Store in an airtight container.

Serve with cheese or cheese spreads, or soft Brie-type cheeses on a cheese board.

## SODA BREAD

*This quick and easy bread does not require rising so it can be prepared, baked and eaten within an hour.*

4 cups flour
1 teaspoon baking soda
1 teaspoon salt,
50 g butter, melted
2 cups buttermilk or plain milk

Mix the flour, baking soda and salt together in a large mixing bowl. Make a well in the centre and pour in the melted butter and milk. Mix to form a soft dough then knead lightly. Shape the dough into an 18–20-cm round. Score the top with a sharp knife and dust with extra flour. Bake in a moderate oven, 180°C, for about 40 minutes. The loaf should sound hollow when the base is tapped. Best served warm.

## BEER BREAD

3 cups flour
3 teaspoons baking powder
1 teaspoon salt
2 teaspoons sugar
375 ml can of beer

Mix all ingredients well. Spoon into a well-greased or non-stick loaf tin, approximately 12×22 cm. Bake at 175°C for an hour. Turn out and cool on a wire rack.

# SPEEDY LUNCHTIME CHEESE ROLLS

3 cups grated cheese
2 cups flour
4 teaspoons baking powder
2 eggs
¾ cup milk

Preheat oven to 250°C. Mix all ingredients together in a large bowl. Drop spoonfuls of the mixture onto a well-greased or non-stick oven tray and place in the hot oven immediately. Make sure you close the oven door as quickly as possible then turn the oven off. Bake for 10 minutes. Remove from oven and cool on a wire rack. Serve warm.

**Makes about 12**

# FARMHOUSE POTATO BREAD

*Moist and light, this is one of the few breads that is even better the day after baking.*

3 large potatoes, peeled and cut into 2-cm
   pieces
2 cups milk
50 g butter, at room temperature
¼ cup sugar
1 tablespoon salt
2 teaspoons dry yeast
5 cups, approximately, all purpose flour

Preheat oven to 200°C. Place potatoes in small saucepan and cover with water. Bring to the boil then simmer until tender, about 10 minutes. Drain. Rub hot potatoes through a sieve into a large bowl.

Combine milk, butter, sugar and salt in heavy small saucepan. Bring to boil, stirring to dissolve sugar. Whisk into potatoes. Allow to cool till just warm, sprinkle yeast over mixture, then stir in. Mix in 4½ cups flour. Knead dough on generously floured surface until smooth and elastic, adding more flour if sticky. Oil a large bowl and roll the dough around in it to coat entire surface. Cover bowl with cling film or a damp tea towel. Allow to rise in a warm, draught-free area until doubled in volume, about 1½ hours.

Remove dough from bowl, punch down and knead until smooth, about 1 minute. Return to bowl. Cover and allow to rise again until doubled in volume, about 1½ hours.

Grease two bread loaf tins. Punch dough down. Cut into two pieces. Shape each piece into a loaf; transfer to prepared tins. Cover tins with tea towels. Allow dough to rise until level with tops of tins, about 45 minutes.

Place bread in preheated oven, reduce temperature to 180°C. Bake until loaves are rich golden brown and sound hollow when tapped, about 30 minutes. Cool in tins for 5 minutes. Transfer to racks and cool completely before serving.

**Makes 2 big loaves**

# P R E S E R V E S

I love to see my pantry bursting with colourful jars. At certain times of the year the garden produces more than we can use and, because I can't bear waste, I turn as much of our produce as possible into jams, chutneys and other preserves. It's also an indication of the "Mrs Squirrel" side of my nature which loves to see food piled up for times ahead.

The other thing about having a good range of preserves on hand is that you can turn the most ordinary, mundane cold cuts into a new culinary experience by adding a special chutney or jelly. Much of my entertaining is done on the "loaves and fishes" principle, i.e. making a little go a long way and, again, the addition of one of my jars, hoarded for these occasions, can make a little go a very long way. This is especially the case in the event of unexpected guests for drinks or dinner. Suddenly, yesterday's leftover chicken can be transformed into pre-dinner nibbles by serving it on ryebread with rosemary jelly. Or as a main course by stir-frying it with some pine nuts, tossing it into a salad and serving it with Pickled Crab Apples. And with a jar or two of Prunes in Port in the cupboard, dessert will never be a problem, either.

Giving a jar or bottle of your home-made preserves to friends makes a very personal present, too. I always see these offerings as "gifts from the heart" as with them goes a little bit of the giver.

# Preserved Aubergine In Olive Oil

*Preserved aubergine slices can be served as a first-course salad with vinaigrette or they can be used as an ingredient for a vegetable gratin or as a topping for pizza or lasagne.*

3 kg medium-sized aubergines, sliced into
    1 cm rounds
½ cup salt
6 cups white wine vinegar
4 cups olive oil
4 teaspoons coriander seeds
2 teaspoons dried chilli flakes

Sprinkle aubergine with salt and spread out in a single layer on a large work surface covered with paper towels. Cover with more paper towels weighted down with a large cutting board or heavy baking trays. Allow to drain for at least 1 hour.

In a large saucepan bring vinegar to the boil, add aubergine slices and bring vinegar back to the boil. Simmer aubergine for 5 minutes, drain and pat dry. Pour 1 cm of oil into sterilised jars and divide aubergine slices among them, sprinkling layers with coriander seeds and dried chilli flakes. Do not pack jars too tightly. Carefully pour oil over the layers, tilting jars so oil seeps right through the layers, covering them completely. Leave a little gap (a few millimetres) at the top of the jars. Seal and store in a cool, dark place for at least one week before using. Store for up to 3 months in the refrigerator.

**Variations:**

Other flavours may be experimented with such as garlic and basil, or rosemary and olives.

***Makes about 4 medium-sized jars***

# Basil And Pine Nut Pesto

*This is a wonderful way to use up copious quantities of summer basil.*

4 cups coarsely chopped fresh basil leaves
1 cup pine nuts
½ teaspoon salt
2 cloves garlic, crushed
½ cup olive oil
½ cup freshly grated Parmesan

In a blender or food processor, purée the basil, pine nuts, salt, garlic and oil, scraping down the sides of the container with a rubber spatula. Transfer the purée to a bowl and stir in the Parmesan. Serve the pesto tossed with pasta or as a sauce for sliced tomatoes or grilled lamb or chicken. Can be frozen, ideally in small portions, for example in ice cube trays.

***Makes about 1½ cups***

# PICKLED VEGETABLES

1 litre white vinegar or cider vinegar
1 tablespoon pickling spice
1 cinnamon stick
¼ cup sugar
optional extras: peppercorns, bay leaf, ginger
3 cups selected mixed vegetables — blanched
  cauliflower, blanched carrot sticks,
  capsicums, button mushrooms, celery,
  baby corn cobs, pickling onions, cucumber,
  shallots, broccoli, baby tomatoes

Place vinegar, pickling spice, cinnamon stick, sugar and any optional extras in a saucepan and heat until boiling. Boil for at least 5 minutes. Strain, or leave spices in vinegar if desired. Cut vegetables into portions or leave whole where applicable. Blanch cauliflower and carrots for 2 minutes only. Firmly pack vegetables into a hot, 1.5-l jar which has been washed, then sterilised in the oven for 15 minutes at 100°C. Pour the hot spiced vinegar over and seal the jar. Leave for at least 6 weeks before eating.

**Makes a 1.5 litre jar**

# PICKLED CRAB APPLES

300 ml cider or white vinegar
500 ml cold water
4 cm piece fresh ginger, sliced
1 cinnamon stick
4 allspice berries
2 cloves
5 cm strip lemon peel
1 cup white sugar
500 g crab apples
bay leaves

Place vinegar and water in a stainless steel saucepan. Add ginger, cinnamon stick, allspice, cloves and lemon peel and bring to the boil. Simmer for 10 minutes. Stir in sugar until dissolved and bring back to the boil. Simmer for 5 minutes.

Meanwhile, wash and drain crab apples. Remove any leaves but keep stalks intact. Steam the fruit, in batches over simmering water, for 8–15 minutes, depending on size, until cooked but not mushy.

Pack the fruit into small, hot, sterilised jars. Add a bay leaf to each jar, placing it against the side of the jar. Strain the boiling syrup on to the fruit. Cover and seal with an airtight lid. Store in a cold place for at least 3–4 days before serving.

**Makes 4 small jars**

# PICKLED WALNUTS

1 bucket (approximately 8 litres) green walnuts
500 g sugar
2½ cups white vinegar
2 teaspoons cinnamon

Soak walnuts in water for 1 week. Change water daily. Boil walnuts until tender. Drain and add sugar, vinegar and cinnamon. Bring to the boil and bottle while hot.

**Makes 6–8 medium-sized jars**

# OVEN-DRIED TOMATOES AND ROASTED CAPSICUMS IN GARLIC BASIL OIL

*2 kg sun-ripened Italian or plum tomatoes*
*8–12 red, green or yellow capsicums*
*10–12 whole heads of garlic cloves, peeled*
*fresh basil leaves*
*oil — preferably extra virgin olive oil or a*
  *mixture of a lighter vegetable oil and olive*
  *oil*

Preheat oven to 100°C. Wash, dry and halve tomatoes lengthways. With a small spoon scoop out the seeds and juice. Cut each half into two lengthways. Place skin-side up on fine meshed wire racks set over the sink for 1 hour, to allow the juice to drain.

Put racks on clean, dry baking trays and place in preheated oven. Dry tomatoes for about 12 hours, turning every few hours until leathery. Remove from oven and allow to cool.

Place capsicums skin-side up on a baking tray and grill until blackened all over. Immediately transfer capsicums to a paper bag or bowl with a lid, to trap the steam. When capsicums are cool enough to handle, rub off the charred skins, and cut into 2 cm strips.

In sterilised jars, layer tomatoes and peppers, placing garlic cloves and basil leaves between the layers, making sure they show against the sides of the jars. Do not pack jars too tightly. Carefully pour oil over the layers, tilting jars so oil seeps right through the layers covering them completely. Leave a little gap (a few millimetres) at the top of the jars. Seal and store in a cool, dark place for at least 1 week before using. Store for up to 3 months in the refrigerator.

***Makes 2 medium-sized jars***

**OVEN-DRIED TOMATOES AND ROASTED CAPSICUMS IN GARLIC BASIL OIL** *are wonderful to eat in a salad, on a pizza or just with crusty bread and cheese. The oil can then be used for making dressings or for basting fish or chicken on the barbecue.*

*Mediterranean flavours are now very much a part of New Zealand cuisine.*

Above: **BASIL AND PINE NUT PESTO** *(page 148) and* **MARINATED OLIVES** *(page 152).*

Right: **FETA CHEESE PRESERVE.**

# FETA CHEESE PRESERVE

*This cheese is great over a crispy spinach salad, grilled on toast, eaten with crusty bread, or as a pizza topping.*

450 g Feta cheese
1 large onion
100 g black olives
few sprigs fresh rosemary
450 ml olive oil, approximately

Cut cheese into cubes. Peel onion and slice into thin rings. Place alternating layers of cheese, olives and onion rings in a medium-sized jar. Add rosemary sprigs and olive oil. Seal the jar and leave to marinate in the refrigerator for at least 3 weeks before serving.

Cheese preserved like this will keep in the fridge for up to three months. As you eat the cheese it can be replaced with fresh cubes. The oil absorbs all the wonderful flavours, so will make a delicious addition to any dressing.

**Makes 1 medium-sized jar**

## LEMON CARDAMON OLIVES

450 g large black olives in brine
rind of 1 lemon, sliced into thin strips
1 tablespoon cardamon seeds
olive oil

Drain and rinse olives. Place in a 500 ml jar with strips of lemon rind and cardamon seeds. Cover with olive oil. Cover and store in a cool place for at least 3 weeks before eating.

## ORANGE AND BASIL MARINATED BLACK OLIVES

*These olives can be used on their own or as an entrée.*

250 g brine-cured black olives, drained and
    rinsed
2 tablespoons olive oil
2 tablespoons fresh orange juice
1 tablespoon minced fresh orange peel
¼ teaspoon crushed red peppercorns, or
    few drops Tabasco
1 tablespoon minced fresh basil

In a medium bowl combine olives, olive oil, orange juice, orange peel and red peppercorns or Tabasco. Cover and store in a cool place for at least 3 weeks before eating.

Before serving, stir in 1 tablespoon minced fresh basil.

**Serves 6**

## TAMARILLO CHUTNEY

2 kg tamarillos, peeled and roughly chopped
1 kg apples, peeled and roughly chopped
1.5 kg brown sugar
750 g onions, peeled and roughly chopped
500 g seedless raisins
1 teaspoon mixed spice
1 tablespoon salt
½ teaspoon cayenne pepper
300 g preserved ginger, roughly chopped
4 cups white vinegar

In a large preserving pan bring ingredients to the boil, stirring, then simmer for 1½ hours. Pour into sterilised jars and seal.

Allow 2–3 weeks for flavours to mature before using.

Note: A very simple sauce can be made by mixing equal quantities of Tamarillo Chutney and sour cream. This is wonderful over plain grilled chicken or used as a creamy medium to mix with chicken pieces, sliced mushrooms, melon cubes, celery and grapes, etc. for a super-easy cold chicken salad.

## CUCUMBER, PINEAPPLE AND MINT PICKLE

*My family's favourite pickle — just scrumptious in cheese sandwiches or with cold meat and salad.*

1 large cucumber or 2 medium-sized
1 cup drained crushed pineapple
3 medium-sized onions, thinly sliced
¾ cup sugar
1 cup white wine vinegar
1½ teaspoons salt
1½ teaspoons curry powder
½ teaspoon turmeric
½ teaspoon celery seed
3 tablespoons chopped mint
1 tablespoon cornflour

Cut cucumber lengthways. Scoop out the seeds and discard. Thinly slice the cucumber with the skin on and place in a large saucepan. Add pineapple, sliced onion and remaining ingredients, except cornflour, to the saucepan. Bring to the boil and simmer uncovered for at least 15 minutes. Mix cornflour with a little water to make a paste and stir into the pickle. Simmer for 3 minutes. Have three or four hot, sterilised jars. Pour pickle in immediately. Use within 6 months.

**Makes 3–4 small jars**

## FEIJOA CHUTNEY

6 cups peeled, sliced feijoas
1 lemon, pips removed, cut up finely, skin and all
1 large onion, peeled and roughly chopped
1 apple, peeled and roughly chopped
1 clove garlic, crushed
60 g sultanas
50 g sliced preserved ginger
1 teaspoon ground cloves
½ teaspoon chilli powder
1 teaspoon salt
2 cups brown sugar
2 cups white wine vinegar

In a large preserving pan bring ingredients to the boil, stirring, then simmer for 1½ hours. Pour into sterilised jars and seal.
   Allow 2–3 weeks for flavours to mature before using.

## HERB JELLIES

*Windfall apples or even apple peelings make excellent jelly which can be flavoured with fresh herbs. These are wonderful accompaniments with roasted meats, game and ham. They look beautiful in old glass jars or cut glass dressing-table pots and make fabulous gifts.*

# APPLE JELLY

*Washed apples, quartered, or apple peelings*
*sugar*
*juice of 1 large lemon*
*a selection of fresh herbs, for example mint,*
*    rosemary, lavender, chive, sage, marjoram*

*It's a great feeling to know that your store cupboard has some of these extra treasures tucked away for when the occasion demands.*

*Pictured here are* **APPLE JELLY**, **PRUNES IN PORT** *and* **APRICOTS IN BRANDY** *(page 157) and* **CUCUMBER, PINEAPPLE AND MINT JELLY** *(page 153).*

Place apples in a large saucepan with cold water to cover. Slowly bring to the boil then turn down the heat and simmer for an hour. Gently mash the fruit as it simmers. Turn off the heat and cool slightly before carefully pouring into a jelly cloth (an old, clean cotton pillowcase is ideal). Suspend the bundle above a wide bowl to catch the drips. Suspending it tied with string to the legs of a chair turned upside-down seems to work well. Leave dripping for several hours or preferably overnight, until all the juice has dripped through. Do not be tempted to squeeze the bag to assist the dripping process, or the jelly will go cloudy.

Discard the apple pulp in the bag. Measure the apple juice into the large saucepan and add 1 cup sugar for every 1 cup of juice. Dissolve over a low heat, then bring to the boil and cook until the temperature reaches 105°C (jelly setting point). Stir in the juice of the lemon and remove from the heat. Pour the apple jelly into small, hot, sterilised jars and add the herbs of your choice. Cover and label the jellies when cold.

### Variations:

- Mint jelly — add finely chopped fresh mint and a drop of green food colouring. Stir the jelly and set aside to cool.
- Rosemary jelly — add 2–3 sprigs fresh rosemary to the jelly and stir well for 2–3 minutes, or until the jelly is nicely flavoured. Remove the sprigs, add a drop of green food colouring and a fresh sprig of rosemary to the jelly. Set aside to cool.
- Lavender jelly — make as for rosemary jelly using fresh flowering spikes of lavender. Omit the colouring. Set aside to cool.
- Sage or marjoram jelly — make as for rosemary jelly.

*Making your own mustard is very satisfying and certainly a lot cheaper than buying it ready made. It's fun to experiment with flavours and little pots of special blend* **GRAINY MUSTARD** *can shorten the 'hard to buy for' Christmas list.*

# GRAINY MUSTARD

½ cup white mustard seeds
¼ cup black mustard seeds
1 tablespoon mustard powder
½ cup white wine or cider vinegar
¼ cup oil
1 teaspoon ground black pepper
¼ teaspoon salt
2 tablespoons flour

In a spice mill or coffee grinder, grind the mustard seeds to the texture of coarse meal. Stir in the ground seed with the mustard powder and vinegar and set aside for 3 hours or overnight, stirring occasionally. Combine mustard mixture with oil and add pepper, salt and flour. Process in a blender until just mixed, for a very grainy mustard, or process a little longer for a more creamy consistency. Store mustard in clean, dry jars, tightly capped. It may be used immediately, but is best left for flavours to develop.

### *Variations:*

To make different flavours, try the following additions to the basic recipe:
• Tarragon and honey
• Horseradish and green peppercorn
• Whisky or brandy, ¼ cup to ¼ cup vinegar
• Lemon — lemon juice and grated zest
• Chilli — chilli powder or sweet chilli sauce
• Herb — 1–2 teaspoons mixed herbs
• Honey — 2 tablespoons honey added before processing

### *Makes 2 small jars*

## C A J U N  S E A S O N I N G  M I X

*Great sprinkled on poultry, fish, shellfish, pork and plain steaks that are going to be grilled or barbecued.*

2 tablespoons salt
2 tablespoons paprika
1 tablespoon garlic powder, granules or flakes
1 tablespoon onion powder, granules or flakes
1 tablespoon ground black pepper
1 teaspoon cayenne pepper
2 teaspoons dried thyme
2 teaspoons dried oregano

Combine all ingredients and store in an airtight container.

## C U R R Y  S P I C E  M I X

*I mix a favourite brand of fairly mild curry powder with these extra spices and herbs to produce a particularly fiery blend that I really enjoy using. Custom-made blends of herbs and spices are lovely personal gifts for friends and perhaps shorten that 'hard to find the perfect gift' list.*

½ cup prepared curry powder
2 tablespoons turmeric
1 teaspoon cayenne pepper
1 teaspoon ground coriander seeds
1 teaspoon ground ginger
2 teaspoons ground chilli
1 teaspoon garlic powder
1 teaspoon finely ground white pepper

Mix all ingredients together and store in an airtight container until required. Use sparingly unless your recipe calls for a generous amount.

# APRICOTS IN BRANDY

*Serve as a dessert with cream, or to spice up a winter fruit salad compôte. Delicious as a side dish with ham or poultry. I often serve brandied apricots as one of the trimmings with my Christmas turkey.*

approximately 24 plump dried apricots
100 g sugar
2 cinnamon sticks
200 ml brandy or to taste

In a medium-sized saucepan place the apricots, sugar and cinnamon sticks. Barely cover with water and gently poach over a low heat for 10 minutes. Drain off the liquid and reserve. Discard the cinnamon sticks. Pack the apricots into a 300 ml sterilised jar and add half the cooking liquid, then top up with brandy. Seal the jar and store in a cool place for 6–8 weeks before eating.

**Makes a 300-ml jar**

# PRUNES IN PORT

*A delicious preserve for an easy dessert, served with lightly whipped cream or sour cream, on tiny plates. These prunes are also fabulous as a side dish in lieu of a sauce with game, poultry, or ham.*

500 g prunes
½ cup sugar
1 cinnamon stick
rind of ½ lemon, cut into strips
1–1½ cups port

Place prunes, sugar, cinnamon stick and lemon rind in a medium saucepan. Barely cover with water and poach for 5 minutes. Pack prunes into a 500 ml sterilised jar. Boil syrup for another 5 minutes to reduce. Pour port over prunes to at least half fill the jar. Pour over the syrup to completely fill the jar. Seal and store in a cool place for at least 3 weeks before eating.

Note: Prunes may be stoned after poaching. Slit lengthways and remove stones before packing into the jar.

**Makes a 500-ml jar**

# INDEX

References to recipes that are illustrated appear in this index in italics.